MIMESIS
INTERNATIONAL

ATMOSPHERIC SPACES
n. 6

ATMOSPHERIC SPACES

Directed by Tonino Griffero

What is an "Atmosphere"?

According to an aesthetic, phenomenological and ontological view, such a notion can be understood as a sensorial and affective quality widespread in space. It is the particular tone that determines the way one experiences her surroundings.

Air, ambiance, aura, climate, environment, genius loci, milieu, mood, numinous, lived space, Stimmung, but also Umwelt, ki, aida, Zwischen, in-between – all these words are names hiding, in fact, the founding idea of atmospheres: a vague ens or power, without visible and discrete boundaries, which we find around us and, resonating in our lived body, even involves us.

Studying atmospheres means, thus, a parte subjecti, to analyse (above all) the range of unintentional or involuntary experiences and, in particular, those experiences which emotionally "tonalise" our everyday life. A parte objecti, it means however to learn how atmospheres are intentionally (e.g. artistically, politically, socially, etc.) produced and how we can critically evaluate them, thus avoiding being easily manipulated by such feelings.

Atmospheric Spaces is a new book series whose aim is to become a point of reference for a community that works together on this philosophical and transdisciplinary subject and for all those whose research, more broadly, is involved in the so-called "affective turn" of the Social Sciences and Humanities.

Meines Radikalismus gegen die psychologistisch-realistisch-introjektionistische Vergegenständlichung, die Weltspaltung und die Menschspaltung in dieser Gestalt, können Sie sicher sein.

Hermann Schmitz.

HERMANN SCHMITZ

NEW PHENOMENOLOGY
A brief introduction

With an introduction by Tonino Griffero

Translated by Rudolf Owen Müllan
with support from Martin Bastert

Original title: Hermann Schmitz, *Kurze Einführung in die Neue Phänomenologie*
© 2014 4th edition Verlag Karl Alber part of Verlag Herder GmbH, Freiburg im Breisgau

This book is published with the support of the GNP and SNP.

© 2019 – Mimesis International
www.mimesisinternational.com
e-mail: info@mimesisinternational.com

Book series: *Atmospheric Spaces*, n. 6

Isbn: 9788869772184

© MIM Edizioni Srl
P.I. C.F. 0241937030

CONTENTS

INTRODUCTION
HOW DO YOU FIND YOURSELF IN YOUR ENVIRONMENT?
Hermann Schmitz's New Phenomenology

By Tonino Griffero

Writing an introduction to an introduction is not always a superfluous exercise. Especially if – as is the case here – the present book cannot do full justice to a wide and ambitious philosophy like that of Hermann Schmitz. Indeed, this text, whose translation will hopefully make New Phenomenology known to a wider scientific (and not only philosophical) community, is a suggestive – but also very brief – presentation of a research that dates back to half a century ago. Take a look at Herman Schmitz's[1] monographs (over fifty, ranging between history and theory) or the intense activity (related to publishing and other things) of the "Gesellschaft für Neue Phänomenologie" (Society for New Phenomenology)[2], a philosophical society founded in 1992 and inspired by his work. And yet it is certainly not the amount of publications that justifies the increasing relevance of an "old-school" philosopher (in the best sense of the expression) like Schmitz. In fact, while maintaining a classical systematic ambition, he proved extremely original in the very personal synthesis he achieved between subjective self-reflection and objective vision (which, besides, was referred to dimensions that cannot be exhaustively defined).

---

1   Not to mention his countless essays. For a complete and updated bibliography of Schmitz (on whom, in general, see Blume 2010) see http://www.gnp-online.de/ Bibliographie-H-Schmitz.18.0.html?&L=%2Fproc%2Fself%2Fenviron. However, as it still is a work in progress – as shown by his numerous recent publications – it is impossible to account for all the aspects of Schmitz's work here (to stick to the partial articulation found in Schmitz 1990, ontology, anthropology, epistemology, theory of time and space, practical philosophy, aesthetics) and for the growing number of philosophical (and interdisciplinary) publications devoted to it.

2   There are many books edited by Gesellschaft für Neue Phänomenologie – first for Akademie Verlag (Berlin) and Koch (Rostock), then for Alber (Freiburg/ München). There are also 28 short books published so far as Rostocker Phänomenologische Manuskripte (ed. by Michael Großheim). Schmitz presented the draft of New Phenomenology in various works (in addition to the volume translated here, Schmitz 2009b, see also 1980c, 1994a, 2003, 2004a).

Other original elements were his jargon, so sophisticated that it sometimes appeared naïve and non-academic[3], and his bibliography, which dared put on the same level canonical authors and – to make an example – obscure military psychiatrists in an open-minded and creative way.

What matters the most, however, is that Schmitz challenges his readers to abandon their prejudices and the artificial ideas prefigured in history, with the aim of changing their way of thinking and help them find a better way of living. Let's face it: even if one is suspicious of the all too frequent new "isms", it is hard to underestimate the theoretical ambition of New Phenomenology. This line of thought, like a new Athena – so to speak – emerged, fully grown and armed, from Schmitz's head (except for its name)[4], finding expression in the *System of Philosophy* (5 vol. in 10 books, between 1964 and 1980, with over 5000 pages)[5] and being increasingly well-received both in philosophy and in other disciplines[6]. Mind you, all of this only happened after decades of disinterest (if not open hostility) of the academic establishment, which was by principle adverse to the systematic voluminosity (regarded as anachronistic) and the explicit aggressiveness (*à la* Nietzsche) of Schmitz's approach. His choice of "non-canonical" topics and references (Theodor Lipps, Richard Avenarius, Rudolf Otto, Ludwig Klages, among others) in an age dominated by Marxism and

---

3   "His work is both the announcement of an influential professor and the pamphlet of an aggressive anarchist" (Soentgen 1998, 175). To reply to the objections contained in Soentgen's useful but only pioneering book, see Schmitz (1999b, 275 ff.).

4   In fact, New Phenomenology is only mentioned for the first time in 1980 (see Schmitz 2009a, 21). The steps towards its fulfillment were: the assumption and expansion of some concepts proposed by Eugène Minkowski (*moi ici maintenant*); b) the development of such notions as "primitive present/presence" and "felt-bodily dynamism"; and, c) finally, their inclusion in the broader concept of "situation" and "state of affairs", as well as the distinction between "identity" and "singularisation". For a summary of the *System*, see Schmitz (1990).

5   See Schmitz (1964, 1965, 1966, 1967, 1969, 1973, 1977, 1978, 1980a, 1980b).

6   By means of its openness, New Phenomenology shows its utility in many applied human sciences (architecture, geography, medicine, phonetics, musicology, psychiatry and psychotherapy, pedagogy, nursing, oriental studies, applied theology, law, management studies, etc.), see Schmitz (2005a) and Werhahn (2011). Provided that it is impossible to account for the countless texts inspired by New Phenomenology and the book series devoted to it by Alber, I wish to refer the reader at least to Schultheis (1998), Moldzio (2004), Schmoll/Kuhlmann (2005), Uzarewicz/Uzarewicz (2005), Großheim (1994, 2008), Koll (2007), Volke (2007), Fehige (2007), Dörpinghaus (2010, 2013), Andermann/Eberlein (2011), Werhahn (2003, 2011), Müller-Pelzer (2012), Gugutzer (2012), Wolf (2012), Becker (2013), Hasse (2005, 2008, 2009, 2012, 2014, 2015), Marcinski (2014) and Nörenberg (2014).

psychoanalysis, hermeneutics, critical theory and structuralism was also met with disapproval, and the same went for his slow and finicky methodology, certainly different from the more popular methodological acrobatics of the time[7].

1. *What Phenomenology?*

Foreign to the widespread "philosophical inhibition to change" (Schmitz 1980c, 9) and to the mirage of reductionism, from the very beginning New Phenomenology aims not only to integrate existing knowledge, but also to "discover" new principles. The idea is to "enhance the quality levels of our life experiences" (Schmitz 1980c, 33), that is to say, all the subtle *chiaroscuro* nuances present in the immediacy of the *Lebenswelt* [lifeworld] that are neglected precisely because they are ubiquitous. In fact, Schmitz immediately focuses on diffuse, undetermined and affective states: in short, the phenomena or appearances that, as Goethe put it[8], are already theoretical despite their ephemeral character and that, as emotionally tuned impressions, are the *prius* of everyday perception. Most of all, those phenomena lie at the heart of the spontaneous (i.e. involuntary) life experience that New Phenomenology takes both as its object of study and as its heuristic method[9], so much so that Schmitz believes he can derive from it power to give direction and content to existence.

> New Phenomenology [...] aims to make their actual lives comprehensible to humans, that is, to make accessible again spontaneous life experience in continuous contemplation after having cleared away artificial ideas prefigured in history. Spontaneous life experience is anything that happens to humans in a felt manner, without their having intentionally constructed it. Today, human thought is so enthralled by seemingly natural assumptions of conventions and hypotheses in the service of constructions that it has become painstaking to disclose spontaneous life experience; but doing so is of great importance, because it can point the way out of dangerous limitations and entanglements of the human understanding of self and world and, in consequence, aid in finding a better way of living (infra, p. 43).

---

7   This method has been rightly compared to not so much a road atlas but rather to a map for pedestrians, which allows one to "discover things to see that standard geography cannot even imagine" (Soentgen 1998, 13).

8   Goethe was already the subject of Schmitz's second book (1959), being the first one on Hegel (Schmitz 1957).

9   Kirchoff (2007, 43).

The centre of the spontaneous life experience is the felt (or lived) body[10], that is, a structure and dynamics that is essentially different from that of the material body (which is made of continuous extension and surfaces). For this very reason, indeed, the felt body is able to certify subjective existence much more than the Cartesian *cogito*. It is precisely thanks to the felt-bodily resonance of experience – which is almost always perfectly expressed by ordinary language – that a person becomes more present to themselves[11], halfway between "understanding and involvement" (Schmitz 2007, 12). Referring to the felt body throughout his whole theory, Schmitz is quite convinced he can offer a way out from the "lazy" scission between technical/scientific rationalism (which is abstract but pragmatically efficient) and pure emotionalism (which is more concrete, but reduced by the prevailing intellectualism to metaphorical irrationality or the so-called culture of fantasy)[12]. In any case, Schmitz's way out does not win over rationalism by finding shelter in an eschatological superillusion whose nihilist presupposition is part of the very problem that utopism itself wants to solve, but by enhancing a counter-world that already exists, even if it is conceptually hard to grasp.

Nevertheless, Schmitz speaks of phenomenology because, rejecting the 20th century philosophical menu[13], he aims to renew the noble but stale phenomenological tradition[14] – which, besides, was responsible for

---

10   Despite being present in every analysis of Schmitz, the topic is mainly addressed in some works (see Schmitz 1965, 1966, 1967, 1985a, 1992, 2007, and especially 2011). For applications of this theory see, among others, Thomas (1996), Gahlings (2006), Uzarewicz (2011), Rappe (1995, 2012), Kammler (2013), Preusker (2014), Julmi (2015, 2017).

11   Schmitz (1980b, 27).

12   European intellectual culture "admits as objective (meaning real) only the already projected objects of handling, planning, reflecting and conforming to an ideal, and privatises as 'merely subjective' that which opposes it, leaving it to poets and edifying orators" (Schmitz 1985b, XVIII). But this subjective sphere, for Schmitz, is less flexible than the philosophical one (Schmitz 1990, 12).

13   "The compact majority of German philosophers currently admits the citation of five philosophers (Kant, Hegel, Husserl, Heidegger and Wittgenstein) and their diadochi and followers; some sectarians add Fichte to the list. In this switching station it is allowed to combine the rails by operating exchanges, but there is no way out" (Schmitz 1994b, XII).

14   Schmitz (1994a, 9). Even Merleau-Ponty merely touched on intellectualist abstractism, ending up being also ensnared in dialectic analogies and transcendental constructivisms (Schmitz 2003, 382-404).

underestimating Rudolf Otto[15] and for other capital sins. In a nutshell, with Husserl it bound subjectivity, yet only transcendentally and positionally understood, to the introjectionist dogma. Also, it reductionistically subordinated the world to intentional acts and intuition of essences on the one hand, and to multiplicity (only numerical and made up of things) on the other, ending up involuntarily becoming "the worst opponent of the phenomenology of the twentieth century" (Schmitz 1996, 561). With Scheler, then, the phenomenological tradition vainly sought a compromise between monist and dualist motives through a vague concept of person. With Heidegger it reductively declassed the diffuse meaningfulness of situations (in *Being and Time*, of course) to an inauthentic reference system, omitting the felt-bodily dimension of our being-in-the-world[16]. Finally, after Heidegger's so-called "turn", it found shelter in "oddities" culminating "in artistic esotericism and political adventurism" (Schmitz 2003, 7, 376)[17].

Thus far the *pars destruens*. On the positive side, New Phenomenology presents itself not as metaphysical or speculative but as empirical knowledge, ontologically tolerant and anti-spiritualist without being materialist, essentialist without being nihilist[18], intentionally and productively naïve in rejecting the transcendental-eidetic approach and the *epoché*[19], while embracing the phenomenological motto "to the things themselves!" Only, this appeal here suggests that one focuses not on the "given"[20] – which

---

15 "The path of phenomenology would have been so much better if Rudolf Otto, the discoverer of the numinous, had been the one to inspire methodic phenomenological objectivity at the time". Otto is considered "a better phenomenologist than Husserl"! (Schmitz 2003, 19-20, 376).

16 Notwithstanding the promising reflection on *Stimmungen* (moods, attunements) in terms of an "ontology of situations (instead of substances with accidents and relations)" (Schmitz 2005a, 72).

17 For a systematic analysis of Husserl and Heidegger see Schmitz (1996).

18 Rather than "thrown" into the world (Heidegger), people are here "carried" by the felt-bodily dynamics and stably "involved" in situations (Soentgen 1998, 179). For an early reflection on nihilism, see Schmitz (1972).

19 "A sudden dissolution of each naive prejudice is impossible if only for the fact that no one fully knows what they believe" (Schmitz 1980c, 21).

20 Because the possibility of "simply keeping one's eyes open to see the real without bias [is] only a regulative principle" (Schmitz 1980c, 25), orientation "to the things themselves" can never be fully realised (Schmitz 1990, 34). It is worth recalling that Schmitz (2014a, 109-115) calls himself a radical evolutionist epistemologist, against both realism – because the world is labile manifoldness, which is given to humans as stable only through the propositional speech – and idealism, if only because humans do not constitute the world,

is always already subsumed in a conceptual and orientative horizon[21] representing its meaning – but on the state of affairs (material or not) whose factuality is evident (but always only for someone and at a time), as it resists all conceivable variations of assumptions required by the individual but not introspective phenomenological revision[22].

In the light of a threefold method, in fact, what is properly real for Schmitz is only the phenomenon or state of affairs that: a) is expressed by a description using ordinary language and non-transcending folk experience; b) results from an analysis aimed at conceptually identifying its salient features without ever eradicating them from the reality of life; finally c) is verifiable by the combinatorial reconstruction of these salient features[23]. Ultimately, what matters is "to gropingly approach what happens to people", that phenomenon that involves them affectively and that therefore "one cannot help admitting" (Schmitz 2005a, 69) – in other words, the state of affairs whose factuality the person cannot in earnest deny.

These phenomena (facts) are real "samples of being" (Schmitz 2005b, 21), endowed with a rich meaningfulness[24] – one that New Phenomenology proves to be irreducible both to subjective projection (constructivism) and to the (Kantian) synthesis of sensible and intellectual. One has to ascertain the "setting in life" of these phenomena[25] without claiming the objectivity required of the natural sciences – as Schmitz repeatedly points out in his criticism of the reductionist-naturalist model. After all, objectivity comes at the cost of reducing the attentional sphere to few types that, because of intermomentary and intersubjective identifiability, measurement and selective variability, are only ideally suited to statistics and experiments and are only used to test theoretical prognoses.

---

but are delivered to it to the extent that they linguistically "derive" it from a primitive and situational present/presence that does not in itself have anything yet of what we call the world.

21   See Schmitz (2005b, 23).
22   Schmitz (1990, 34; 2002, 20; 2003, 1). Given this evidence, no one "could any longer have self-confidence if they contested its [of that state of affairs] existence" (Schmitz 2005b, 26).
23   Schmitz (1990, 33; see also 1992, 30-31).
24   Supporting the primacy of *Bedeutsamkeit* [meaningfulness], Schmitz evidently follows one of his masters: Erich Rothacker.
25   Schmitz (1994a, 7).

Against the triumphal march of this reductionism (from Plato to today's world wide web) Schmitz sets an archaic paradigm, which after the 5th century B.C. only survived in minority and heterodox enclaves (Neo-Platonism, Pythagorean numerology, humoral medicine, astrology, mysticism, natural magic, Paracelsianism, alchemy, popular philosophy, etc.). Schmitz regards this paradigm a bit as Goethe (1998, nr. 662) regards the Homeric poems: that is, as the "most delightful and ideal state of nature", thanks to which such a paradigm seems "to deliver us, if only for brief moments, from the fearsome load with which tradition has weighed us down over many thousands of years". In particular, this forgotten paradigm represents "a basis of abstraction that is closer to life experience compared to what has governed the prevailing intellectual culture in Europe ever since Democritus, Plato and Aristotle" (Schmitz 2007, 15). Its almost total and tragic extinction (which can be dated between 450 and 350 b. C.) is for Schmitz the cause of pretty much all the missteps of the history of the Western culture and their obvious consequences: the weakening of superindividual spheres (the cultures of law and religion, for example) and collective situations (rooted in a *nomos*)[26] in favour of an autistic-individual fragmentation and an irresponsible ironic scepticism; the uncritical acceptance of the dogma of immanence, resulting in room for solipsistic hedonism (simplified in terms of pleasure/displeasure); and the intensification of the processes of self- and world-empowerment (theological but also technological)[27].

The rehabilitation of this archaic dynamism means emphasizing the *logos* presupposed by the felt-bodily feeling, that is, an embodied alphabet that allows one to relativise many of the traditional notions (soul, creativity, etc.), which prove to be phenomenologically unjustified artificial constructs. In fact, when for the philosopher calmly sat in his armchair matters get serious, and their felt body takes over the incorporeal self-reference dear to traditional philosophy, their reflection ceases to be

---

26 Indeed, Plato's Socrates, significantly deaf to the constraints of relevant situations, already appears committed to dissolving them in a constellationistic way. On collective life-feelings see Großheim/Kluck/Nörenberg (2014).

27 Monotheism itself would be functional to the control of a divine atmosphericness, originally more varied and disturbing (Schmitz 1977, 177). The final outcome of the "dynamistic" mistake would be Hitler and the atom bomb (Schmitz 1997, 211): two phenomena explained as overcompensating the spirituality deficits of the West (Schmitz 1999; in sum 2010a, 127-130). For a criticism, cf. Landkammer (2000) and Heubel (2003).

a speculative construction of the universe and becomes an introspective awareness of how one finds themselves in his environment[28]. In other words, one starts analysing what they "feel" felt-bodily after a certain irritation or incertitude (*Beirrung*) related to the – no longer obvious – process of finding themselves[29]. Note how, in Schmitz, Platonic wonder takes the form of the most dramatic amazement for meanings that suddenly turn out to be illusory. From this original affection – obviously in a rigorous and critically founded (but not deductive) linguistic form – arise all the great philosophical questions, as such inaccessible to hard sciences[30], whose best synthesis is: "what phenomenon asserts itself as a fact?"; "of what suggested state of affairs can I not seriously (in good conscience) deny that it is a fact?".

Instead of articulating itself in the usual sectorial specialisations, Schmitz's philosophy appears also as a "descriptive metaphysics"[31], far from the necessarily constructionist and prognostic claims of causal and genetic explanation, but also aware (unlike a certain proto-phenomenological "nudism") that it can never be separated from the filter of pre-figured and salient perspectives provided by a nonetheless necessary basis of abstraction. What Schmitz radically opposes, therefore, is thus not abstraction *tout court*, but only the selective abstraction implied by the predominance of the psychologistic-reductionist-introjectionist paradigm[32]. In fact, the objectification produced by this paradigm defines the most diverse everyday life experiences and nuances as "nothing-but" – this is the essential meaning of every reductionism – reducing them to physical data in the natural sciences, to language in analytic philosophy and, now, to the brain in neuroscience. In particular, the neuroscience is contradictorily forced to account for the "ecological" perceptions it wishes to reduce to physical signals formed at a neural level[33], in addition to

---

28 This is the guiding principle of all philosophy, for Schmitz (1964, 14-27; 2018, 25 ff.).
29 There is philosophy only where there is this irritation, therefore for Schmitz the philosopher is a sort of "born" neurotic.
30 For example: What concerns me? What should I really take seriously? What can I overlook? What am I capable of? And so on.
31 Based on reviewable concepts nonetheless, unlike what happens in Strawson (Werhahn 2011, 11-12).
32 Hence, generally speaking, Indo-Germanic syntax, post-Democritean metaphysics and an ontology reductively founded on things, properties and relations (Schmitz 2005b, 19).
33 On perception conceived, on the contrary, as felt-bodily communication with rich impressions cf. Schmitz (1978; 2002, 54-64; 2007, 28-45; 2010b, 120-132),

doubting whether to consider the brain a simple medium or to "pretend" that it is an apparatus consciously able to produce meanings[34]. Naturalistic reductionism, the corollary of an epochal division of the world, thus loses sight of real sensible experience, both phenomenal and affective, paving the way to a history of "repressions" that it is necessary to fix.

2. *A (non) Felix Culpa: The Psychologistic-Reductionist-Introjectionist Paradigm*

Neither so archaeological as to simply interpret the philosophers of the past to make their theories seem less stupid, nor so anachronistic as to escape the challenge of their contextual reconstruction, New Phenomenology has the merit of always accompanying its own investigation of phenomena with a fierce determination of the errors of the past. As Schmitz believes it is perfectly legitimate to engage in dialogue with, say, Plato and Aristotle[35], both on their problems and solutions and on the epochal (also historical-political) effects of their ideas, his work escapes the narrow definition of historical-philological specialism[36]. Indeed, in relation to history of philosophy, Schmitz's thought provides a suggestive narrative *geistesgeschichtlich*, able to give an adequate re-orientation on the meaning of life. At times it coincides with tradition, at times it distances itself from it – in any case, this narration compensates for the disorienting effect of modernisation while always philologically justifying phenomenological research.

Let's leave aside here the historical-political background of this analysis[37], as well as the polemical idea that nothing truly new was ever conceived after Neo-Platonism. Instead, let's focus on the "mother" of all mistakes – that is, the above mentioned psychologistic-reductionist-introjectionist paradigm – and its consequences (dynamicism, autism, ironism). Let's

---

and then, on the background of New Phenomenology, Kluck/Volke (2012) and Kluck's wide research (2014).

34 Hence the grotesque conclusion (for Schmitz) that life experiences allegedly are a causal product of the brain. See Schmitz (2002, 99-112; 2014a, 126-130).

35 Analysed in three thick books (Schmitz 1985b).

36 This imposes not to describe a past author's thought according to criteria (concepts and language) that weren't available at their time.

37 Schmitz looks favourably, for example, at the aftermath of the reunified Germany, the recovery of Eastern Christianity and especially the idea, attributed to neo-Platonic sources, of *sobornost* or organic solidarity (Schmitz 1999, 396-404).

start from the beginning. Schmitz (ironically?) states to oppose not the whole history of philosophy but "only" the thought that followed the pre-Socratics, dominated by abstraction and by a dogmatisation of fictional hypotheses[38] still present in the (experimental-statistical-combinatorial) *forma mentis* of contemporary physics, which broke free from any previous transcendent delegation only thanks to modern mathematisation. The entire Western culture would be indeed guided by a mistake made by the Greeks, after they emerged victorious in the war with the Persians and took the path of science, aesthetics and democracy.

In this critical genealogy, the first thinker to blame is Democritus[39]: he is responsible for replacing dynamism with kinetics, for intra-human dualism between soul (thought of as a material house for the first time) and the material body declassed to the former's tool, and for the reductionist standardisation of the features of atoms, conceivable as stable invariants in the incessant flow (hence also the contraposition between matter and form) just like Platonic ideas. This fatal paradigm turn – a forced change of direction, if we assume, with Schmitz, the rail junction model – caused the genesis of a thought that has three main features. First, it is combinatory-prognostic because it is based on singularisation, that is, the nominalist dogma that everything is singular[40]. Second, it is constructivist because it rests on projectivism, that is, the idea that outside meaningfulness is but the outcome of a human projection (even pragmatically conditioned) – a prejudice become virulent in Nietzscheanism – on a world made up of mere quantitative elements. Finally, it is constellationist, based on an understanding of the world as a network of individual (singular) factors.

Plato himself is allegedly but an epigone of this fatal turn[41], even if he became a sort of *spiritus rector* of what followed. Aristotle opposed Plato, but nevertheless was responsible for other serious mistakes, such as the elaboration of a tripartite ontology (things-properties-relations) as opposed to Platonic ideas. The problem with Aristotle's ontology is mainly that it disclaims all that exists despite not being any of the mentioned three terms, and does not provide the priority of relations with respect to the *relata*. As we know, this turn – which is anthropological-pedagogical rather

---

38   Schmitz (1999, 377).
39   See Schmitz (2003, 333-348).
40   Singular is what increases a number by 1 within a finite set or genus (already given).
41   See Schmitz (2003, 348-363).

than strictly theoretical, as it is due to the human need for self-and world-empowerment, which stylises the human being as an autonomous person no longer subject to the arbitrary tyranny of external forces – is opposed by Schmitz through archaic felt-bodily dynamism[42]. Instead, the latter can still be found in the Pythagoreans' dynamics of polarity; in Empedocles' idea of the conflict of love and anger as spatially extended atmospheres; in Aeschylus' conception of resentment as a superpersonal atmospheric mood; in Heraclitus' metaphorical contraposition between bow and lyre; but also, residually, in the stoic doctrine of the dynamics of the *tonos* (exemplified by the lived body) and even in St Paul's idea of spirit and flesh as conflicting atmospheric forces in the human body.

For Schmitz, who objected to the hypothesis of a Homeric unitary psychology and anthropology, the best example of such "antelapsarian" *forma mentis* lies in the *Iliad*[43]. This (non philological) Homer, for whom human beings are exposed to the obsession or affection of gods[44], sees human life experiences as not purely psychic: they are a dimension still decentred and exposed without protection to a "concert of semi-autonomous sources of impulse, the most important of which is *thymós*" (Schmitz 2003, 342). Life experiences are not only psychophysically undifferentiated as still related to an image of the world that prefers the distinction between organ and its function over the dualism between body and spirit (or soul); in Homer they are mostly the example of an age that explains everything on the basis of felt-bodily impulses and not the differentiation of the organs of sense. At that time, all that would later be defined "psychic" was taken to be felt-bodily with the same one-sidedness with which Modernity would make the body psychic in every respect. Homeric times relied on a perceptual body schema (the habitual conception of one's own body) that modern psychology would derive from the experiences made through the senses, to which Schmitz opposes a felt-bodily motor schema, based on the irreversible directions and on the swaying of diffuse felt-bodily islands[45].

And yet things changed already in the *Odyssey*. Here, in the frame of a struggle between *psyché* and *thymos*, the hero (who in this sense is already

---

42   See Schmitz (1988a, 1988b).
43   See Schmitz (1965, 365-445).
44   In this sense complexes (Freud) and archetypes (Jung) are allegedly similar to Homeric impulses, while lacking a felt-bodily localisation (Schmitz 1990, 200).
45   See Schmitz (2011, 21-23). On felt-bodily islands see Griffero (2017a, 55-67; 2016b).

fully modern)[46] can already distance himself from his and outer felt-bodily impulses, exerting complete control over them as well as over his facial expression. In Odysseus, personal emancipation runs now parallel to his rationalism that declasses the divine-numinous to a *daimon*, reduced to a predictable partner (who, in any case, can be begged); its most harmful consequence is the introjection of feelings into a closed-off inner sphere[47]. The latter then appears to be conceived as a solid body: a metaphorical multistory house (mind, reason, intellect, senses) furnished with all the meaningfulness (intentional acts, ideas, memories, impulses, sensation, feelings) that, before, was mistakenly taken away from the external world and is now believed to be governed by reason.

This privatisation of the emotional sphere continued, made easier by the progressive disappearance of transcendent restraints and fears. In the Christian Middle Ages (for Schmitz, 313-1303 a. C.) it also involved the believers' happiness, as they had to control the drives of a body already reduced to a machine (Augustine). Then it gave rise to a singularist ontology (Ockham) for which reality, made up of singular and discrete entities, lends itself to the most arbitrary constellationistic combinations, producing, as its ultimate consequence, technical expertise, the market economy and even today's computer digitisation. In parallel, the power of affective involvement, first attributed solely to God, then moved on to Western Christianity, through various compromises and de-mystification (papacy, the Crusades, imperialism, etc.) aimed at adapting the divine to man's needs, even placing it in the hands of the latter. And that, for Schmitz, says enough about the – no longer only elitist-aristocratic – strive for self-control and the search for a no longer transcendent, but earthly wellbeing (capitalism).

3. The "Cabinet of Errors" and (Possible) Therapies

Thus far I have reconstructed the historical advent of the fatal psychologistic-reductionist-introjectionist paradigm. Now the point is to examine the repressions due to that advent, which took as obvious the idea that the only possible feelings are human and the only possible meanings

---

46   Note that this reconstruction (Schmitz 1965, 445-451; 1969, 413-418) is
      independent and yet largely similar to that of Adorno and Horkheimer.
47   As for his criticism of introjection, albeit with different arguments, Schmitz, also
      refers to Avenarius (1912).

of the world are constructed by humans and projected on the outside – this idea is undoubtedly the number one enemy of New Phenomenology.

A. The first repression regards the body, degraded from felt or lived body (*Leib*) − whose felt-bodily voluminosity was (and is) experienced independently of the spatial and physic dimension – to a material-anatomic body (*Körper*), understood as spatially and physiologically delimited, perceptible from the outside and arbitrarily manipulable. With the success of the dualism between soul (unextended) and material body (extended), the felt body ceases to be what it was in ancient Greece[48] and, as a sinking stream, even in Christian anthropology before its surrender to Platonism. That is, it ceases to be whatever someone feels in the vicinity (not always within the boundaries) of their material body as belonging to themselves, without drawing on the five senses (in particular, sight and touch) as well as the perceptual body schema. Thus, the body ceases to be a "crowd" of felt-bodily islands that – unable to be exactly located – come and go, become obtrusive, and recede into the background again. Such islands are sometimes relatively stable (oral cavity, anal zone, chest, back, belly, genitals, soles, etc.), while at other times they come forward or dissolve on the basis of excitement (itch, palpitation, burst of heat, ache, etc.). In any case, they generate in the felt body a constant intracorporeal communication. Without this lived body, the outside world becomes accessible only through the senses, entrusted with the task of deciphering, combining and capitalizing on the signals that are supposed to come to the inner world and to therein be able to form an acceptable image of the outside world.

At the same time, one fact, absolutely crucial to understand the real situation of mankind, is obviously disregarded: the felt body constantly generates a ubiquitous embodied communication with the outside world thanks to bridging qualities that can be felt in one's own lived body but can also be perceived in encounters with other things and persons, whether at rest or in motion. Such a felt-bodily communication[49] varies depending on the form of binding of the two poles of vital drive (tightness/wideness)[50]. It also

---

48   But not only: for a look at other cultures, see Rappe (1995).

49   See Schmitz (1978, 75-109; 1989, 175-217; 2002, 54-64; 2005c, 168-184; 2011, 29-53; 2016, 183-210; 2017, 64-79). Let me also refer to Griffero (2016b; 2016d; 2017b).

50   The different intertwinement of the two extreme poles produces all other polarities, such as contraction/expansion, tension/swelling, up to the extremes of privative contraction due to a fright (and therefore impotence), and of privative expansion due to falling asleep or dozing off (for instance after orgasm). See,

changes depending on whether the felt body, by means of privative expansion and privative contraction, aims towards expandedness or contractedness[51].

Now unable to understand the absolute and affective location of the felt body (by means of irreversible directions) and the potentialities of their being-in-the-world thanks indeed to ubiquitous felt-bodily communication (whose driving forces are encorporation and excorporation), Western culture has solely focused on the physical body[52]. The latter is placed in a locational and relative space by means of mutual determination aided by positions and distances. It is a material body so quantifiable in an object-like way that it can be perfectly described in the third person perspective. Constructed on the basis of surfaces – in which there are points that can be connected by reversible lines – the material body has to imply, in turn, a single locational space, now radically foreign to the more original surfaceless and predimensional space of the felt-body[53].

B. The second repression – also connected to psychosomatic dualism and, if you like, to the so-called "discovery of the mind" (Bruno Snell) following the oblivion of the felt body – concerns feelings and their specific spatiality. In fact, psychologism consists precisely in translating/reducing the entirety of personal experience to the psyche (or soul, *mens*, mind, conscience, and today especially brain): that is, to a closed-off private inner sphere. Instead, New Phenomenology frees emotions and feelings from their introjection into the soul and considers them as felt-bodily moving forces that are spatially poured out in a lived, pre-dimensional, pre-geometrical and surfaceless space (like that of sound, of weather, of posture, etc.). This is how Schmitz philosophically inaugurated – then followed also by

---

amongst others, Schmitz (1965, 73-172; 1966, 7-36; 1993, 115-149; 2005c, 150-155; 2011, 15 ff.).

51   Unlike the Freudian impulse, this felt-bodily dynamics is non-objectual and non-finalistic, so much so that the following unity is allegedly never static or perfect, but "cruel" (Schmitz 1965, 326) because of its constantly conflicting nature.

52   While opposing this reductionist turn, Schmitz (only) initially admits that, in addition to two ontologically different dimensions such as the felt body (the very topic of phenomenology) and the material body (object of the natural sciences), there is also an intermediate one (lived-material body), made up precisely of the islands whose localisation is both absolute and relative, acting as the intersection of the two areas.

53   See Schmitz (especially 1967, 1969; 2005c, 185-217), Landweer (2008) and, for the relation between space levels and types of atmospheric feelings, Griffero (2014a).

Gernot Böhme[54] and others – a thematisation of atmospheric feelings that today raises growing scientific (and interdisciplinary) attention[55]. Accordin to him, they can be pure moods (contentment and despair *in primis*) or centred excitements; but what matters for New Phenomenology is to reiterate that feelings and emotions are not mainly private states of the soul but atmospheres. In other words, they are non-physical forces – in many ways analogous to the primal images (*Urbilder*) conceived by Ludwig Klages[56] as daemonic powers – that cannot be explained as intentional acts. In fact, Schmitz reinterprets this supposed intentionality in the terms of Gestalt psychology (Wolfgang Metzger), distinguishing within emotions a region of density (where their characteristic features are gathered) and an anchoring point (from which they issue forth as gestalt).

In a nutshell, atmospheres are centripetal and external vectors; they have authority and, generating affective involvement (an embodied experience), they grip the vital drive, suddenly taking over and leaving the perceiver based on their specific resonance[57] in their personal embodied disposition. For the ancients, rage, *eros* and parrhesia – for instance – were not private inner emotions but atmospheres, partially personified respectively by Ares, Aphrodite and the Holy Ghost. Also, they were taken to be so external as to be impervious to the human projective impulse, while today such impulse is regarded as constructivistically omnipotent, leading to the erroneous belief that the world is semantically and affectively empty[58]. Be they swift

---

54   See Böhme (1989, 1995, 1998, 2001, 2006, 2017a, 2017b, 2017c).
55   The theme recurs in many writings by Schmitz. The main ones are Schmitz (1969, 91 ff.; 1977, 74-134; 2002, 65-76; 2003, 243-261; for a recent summary 2014b). It is also interesting to look at Fuchs' take on this (2000, passim) and Schmitz's replies (2003, 175-205; 2005c, 270-276). On atmospheres, I refer the reader also to some of my works which are translated into English: see Griffero 2013, 2014a, 2014b, 2014c, 2014d, 2016a, 2016b, 2017a, 2018a). For a more comprehensive bibliography (*in fieri*), see the dedicated website I am in charge of: https://atmosphericspaces.wordpress.com.
56   On Schmitz's relation with Klages, whom he considered "the closest of my kindred spirits" (Schmitz 1992, 258), see Schmitz (1992, 255-287) and, more generally, Grossheim (1994). Cf. also Griffero (2016c).
57   The relative subjectivity of atmospheric perception (Schmitz 1990, 310) can therefore be explained starting from the different embodied disposition (bathmothymic, cyclothymic, schizothymic) and the different relation between personal idiosyncratic world and personal alien world (so that a person can be, say, extrovert, introvert and ultrovert).
58   Some have objected that atmospheres thus risk being reified (Hauskeller 1995, 21-31; Soentgen 1998, 59, 106-110) and the subject risks being discharged, as a

or gradual, atmospheres govern our thymic life. In fact, it is undoubtedly true that we can have the mere perception of an atmosphere without being in the grip of it, and it can even happen that an emotion (as an atmosphere) is in the air without anyone feeling it; however, atmospheres normally grip a person as half-entities (quasi-things or half-things)[59], thus arousing a natural and very precise suggestion of motion, luckily not yet fully repressed by our personal emancipation[60].

For Schmitz, as we have seen, the capital sin is introjection. If "for every individual endowed with conscience, the world is split between their own external and internal worlds, with the proviso that they will become maximally aware of an object of their own external world only insofar as such object has a proper representation within the internal world of the individual" (Schmitz 2007, 14), then it is inexplicable how the subject can "leave" such a prison house (box) – closed off to the outside world and hierarchically articulated in layers ever since Plato – and access the outside world. As we have seen, this view (which was born and consolidated starting from the 5th century B.C.) of the soul as a substantial support of all life experiences relieves humans from the dictates of atmospheric feelings, making them independent for the first time and therefore ethically-criminally liable for what previously could be attributed to transcendent forces. Hence it is the doubling, in the soul, between subject and object – think of the Platonic *topos* of thinking as the soul soliloquizing within the soul – that for Schmitz equals to say (contradictorily) that an inhabitant of a house is also the house in which he lives. Following the introjection of external emotions (atmospheres),

---

mere "passenger of atmospheres" (Soentgen 1998, 117). I have tried to reply to such objections both on a phenomenological and on an ontological level (Griffero 2017a, 19-53).

59   Quasi-things (for example: human voice, wind, sense of gravity, pain, melodies, rhythms, night, time, etc.) differ from full-things because of their intermittency – they appear and disappear, but we cannot sensibly ask ourselves where they have gone and how they have existed in the meantime – and because they do not have a three-polar causality (cause-influence-effect) but a bi-polar one (cause/influence-effect), as there is no autonomous cause prior to their influence. I have proposed elsewhere a first systematisation of an ontology of quasi-things such as pain, shame, gaze, twilight among others (cf. Griffero 2017a).

60   "The way in which the feelings take possession of the felt body can be both a tacit creeping and a sudden and violent infestation [...] But this in no way changes the mimic certainty described. The doubts about what is the feeling that really grips us is not at all uncertainty about the choice of gestures" (Schmitz 2002, 73-74).

the world appears neutralised and tragically devoid of all that pathically "moves" human beings; on the other hand, the soul, thus closed-off, turns into a black box from which the five senses escape always only "on parole", testifying the outside world in a weak way.

The possibility of self- and world-empowerment comes at a dear price. The destruction of collective situations produces, first of all, the disconsolate autism (social atomism) that legitimates Hobbes' *homo homini lupus* and is only partially compensated by a conventional sociality (Protestant world), and active-mannerist one (Catholic-Jesuit world) or one that sticks to ceremonies like the *ancien régime*. Love, too, loses its once indispensable ideal anchoring point (the beauty, virtue and decency of the loved one), turning into a passion free of external legitimacy and exclusively oriented to pleasure[61]. Insecurity and self-alienation were initiated by the French Revolution and by the thought of Fichte, for whom the floating of imagination above or between all facts has a great "career" in the Romantics (mainly Novalis and F. Schlegel), persuaded to be able to turn "away from" anything (recessive irony) and "to" anything (productive irony). Even Hegel admits to this, convinced that "everyone will [...] find in himself the ability to abstract himself from all that he is, and in this way prove himself able of himself to set every content within himself"(Hegel 1821, 30).

This ironic-nihilistic oscillation – which explains today's search for superficial experiences (in private life, the media, sport, tourism, etc.) and only offers situations that are no longer seriously involving – pushes modern, frustrated human beings in two directions: on the one hand, they obsessively look for something to hold on to in the hope to regain some "place in the cosmos" (state, society, Christianity, logical order, common sense, Being, etc.); on the other, they would arbitrarily enact any role to impress others without being impressed themselves (think of dandies)[62]. For Schmitz, this ironic dandyism has a philosophical face, which can even be found in Wittgenstein's *Tractatus*: in fact, assuming that there only are objective facts, he claims that what we cannot speak about (but isn't this the most important life experiences?) we must pass over in silence. However, it also has a popular face: that of letting oneself go to the increasing amount of technological devices and arrogantly aiming at self-realisation: "as if a self that can be realised were already undoubtedly present" (Schmitz 2010a, 126).

---

61   See Schmitz (1993; 2005, 99-111).
62   Schmitz (2010a, 111-126).

C. The third repression, perfectly consistent with the oblivion of the pathic and external sphere in its reductionism, concerns the outside world. The latter has been understood based on the generalisation of a rare circumstance: the calculation of solid bodies at the centre of the visual field[63]. Mostly, the outside world has been physically "reduced" to a few selected and standard types, which can be exactly measured and are functional to the predictive power of hypotheses, as well as to the fact that man can (or believes he can) take power into his own hands. After Democritus, external impressions (the so-called secondary and tertiary qualities[64], the heart of uncontrollable life experiences, atmospheres, the sources of suggestions of movement, synaesthetic qualities and felt-bodily communications)[65] were either exiled into (aestheticising) irrelevance, or converted by force and with grotesque results in full-things, as when the wind (a quasi-thing) is reinterpreted as air in motion.

D. The last repression can be also attributed to the phenomenological mainstream and concerns situations[66]. The perceptual *prius* of our everyday life is an internally diffuse meaningfulness in the sense that, within it, not everything (possibly nothing) is singular. More precisely, situations are made up states of affairs (something is the case), programmes (something ought to/should be the case) and/or problems (whether something is or not). Their chaotic non-numerical manifoldness – that is, their undecidedness about identity and difference – is only overcome when (eventually) situations become the object of a prosaic explication, which is as such more coarse[67] than a poetic one (broadly understood) and, for this very reason, suitable for singularisation. However, what matters for New

---

63   Schmitz (1990, 21).
64   On the contrary, for Anaximenes, Parmenides and Empedocles, knowledge also implied the observation of significant impressions.
65   Schmitz (1966) also explains the evolution of styles in architecture and figurative arts with the becoming of these felt-bodily elements.
66   The notion of "situation" concretises, from a point in the *System* onwards (Schmitz 1977), the more primal notion of "chaotic": it is worth noting that the latter concept was still thematised by Schmitz long before it became a customary topic of the natural sciences (see Gamm 1994, 73 ff., and for a defence against his objections, see Soentgen 1998, 152).
67   "The prosaic explication […] aims to isolate in a situation states of affairs (relevant facts) and privileged programmes (ready for decision), while throwing away all the rest" (Schmitz 1994b, 237).

Phenomenology is that, even if the analysis solves the initial vagueness[68] and singles out the meanings that were previously a subtle part of the internally diffuse meaningfulness of situations, it must never be more fine-grained than necessary – otherwise what follows is the pathological and unscientific pedantry to want to know exactly what one has competence in without analytical knowledge (*je-ne-sais-quoi*)[69].

Situations can be of different kinds: impressive or segmented (depending on whether the whole meaning or only part of it shows), current or long-standing (depending on whether the changes can be observed in the short or long run), private or collective, etc. They appear as rich and polysignificant impressions, also in the sense that they make an impression on someone and "purport more than one might say individually" (Schmitz 1994a, 13), especially of course to those who have the (for Schmitz, very "womenly") talent to understand similarities and ambivalences not deductively[70]. By introducing the concept of situation, Schmitz feels he has a tool to reconsider some now unproductive notions: in fact, the "soul" becomes the phenomenologically more accessible personal situation; the "moral conscience" turns out to be only the residual form of the external pathic sphere a situation consists of; finally, the Platonic theory of ideas (which, as such, are not criteriologic)[71] should be regarded not so much as a positivistic compensation for metaphysics – as Heidegger thinks – but rather as the reductionist version of atmospheric feelings and significant situations.

The neo-phenomenologist, now we know, wants to shed light – reflective, but as contiguous as possible to life – on an affective involvement that, unlike shadows projected on the wall (Plato), should not be sacrificed to the benefit of sunlight (abstract ideas). If anything, such an involvement is to be understood, and that's why Schmitz – who devoted himself to philosophy "also" because of the emotional shock of Nazism[72] – finds a common thread between the three abovementioned mistakes (autism,

---

68   Exaggerating the vagueness of feelings, in any case, seems to Schmitz like a reflection of the mistaken introjectionist conception of affective life (Schmitz 1999b, 288).

69   See Schmitz (2014a, 77-78).

70   See Schmitz (1980a, 379; 1993, 85-86).

71   In Plato there is "beauty, which is nothing but beautiful [and] goodness, which is nothing but good" (Schmitz 1999b, 392).

72   See Schmitz (1999a, 9-10).

dynamicism[73], ironism) that even leads to Hitlerism[74]. Or, more precisely, it leads to "disposing, in technical and mass form, of death for death's sake through the means of modern technology" (Schmitz 1999a, 53) through which a rationalistic and hypertrophic dynamicism (mistakenly) believes to prevail over autistic deviation.

As you can see, in this critical genealogy and history of orientation, Schmitz is not contented with studying temporarily circumscribed conceptual cores, but – hermeneutically "examining" the past starting from "our" problems – he suggests a wide-ranging overhaul of the traditional way of thinking. Mostly, he doesn't merely diagnose historical-spiritual mistakes[75]: he also proposes a therapy. The dynamistic error is treatable through the (re)discovery of primitive present/presence as the centre of an existence without utopian alibis. The autistic error is treatable theoretically through the repudiation of nominalism and constellationism; it requires deep implanted situations[76] to be regenerated in a superpersonal nomos and in atmospheric feelings that free their bearers from the disorienting freedom of indifference. Finally, the ironist error is fixable thanks to the discovery of radically subjective facts, which I'll talk about now.

---

73   This relatively excludes – hence a less systematic push to self- and world-empowerment – both the Eastern Church, influenced by the writings of St John and Neo-Platonism, and Islam, for which divine power remains very unpredictable (Schmitz 1999a, 42).

74   Going through Baconian triumphalism, Lutheran individual salvation, the combination of technique and imperialism, intramundane asceticism, the oblivion of practical and ethical habitualities, and last but not least autism, poorly compensated in totalitarianism (and in the phobic-Faustian anti-triumphalism specific of Hitler) by the identification in collective destiny favoured by a subtle technique of impressions.

75   For a hypersynthetic version see Schmitz (1999a, 390-396).

76   Schmitz mentions Confucian ethics, foreign to the Hegelian dualism of ethics and morality, but rigorously condemns any artificially homogeneous situation (from Jacobin stagings to Nazi parades). This explains why, despite his conception of art in terms of "distanced involvement" and controlled cultivation of atmospheric feelings (1990, 455-497; 2007, 81-93; 2012, 188-192), he believes, *contra* Böhme's aesthetics, that what can be intentionally produced are not atmospheres but only impressions of propaganda (Schmitz 2003, 256). This is a land where those of us who profess a pathic aesthetics (see Griffero 2016a, 2017b), obviously cannot follow him.

4. *The (Re)discovery of (Absolute) Subjectivity*

When we get up from our armchair to reflect philosophically on the concrete terrain of life experiences[77], we immediately notice – in a rather painful way – that feelings and emotions do not segregate us in a closed-off inner world. Yet, in his crusade to externalise the affective, Schmitz vigorously and without contradiction supports also the salience of subjectivity[78]. The felt-bodily and affective involvement, in fact, ensures the existence of something much more than the objectivity achieved by successive abstractions ever could, but it also ensures subjectivity much more than the *cogito*, deceptively believed to be free of doubt. But what is being considered here is only a strict and absolute subjectivity[79], conceived of not as ineffable knowledge about one's own private inner sphere, but as the indispensable presupposition also of descriptive third-person objectification.

The qualifying point is the ontological, and not just epistemic, distinction between subjective facts and objective facts. That is, respectively: the meanings that one person at most can talk about (using their own name), and those that everyone can talk about (and merely name), insofar as they know enough and have the language skills. "The subjective does not consist [...] in a position on the terrain of objective facts (relational subjectivity) but in a different kind of factuality: the factuality of subjective facts for someone" (Schmitz 2005a, 6). In fact, only subjective facts or meanings affect us closely and grip us through and through, expressing what we really are and making us (when we don't ignore them, that is) conscious subjects – regardless of whether such facts precede their neutralisation into objective facts or whether the latter are rather going through a (healthy and providential) moment of crisis. Thus involved, the subject can say "I" with a surplus of meaning that is always affective-embodied and not banally content-related; for this very reason, despite the insurmountable incompleteness of the self[80], neutral facts completely lack such a surplus. Only subjective facts (which are "facts" in the full sense precisely because they are more indisputable and urgent than, say, a mathematical fact)[81]

---

77 For an attempt to apply the main neophenomenological concepts to everyday life see Keller (2013).
78 He does this from the beginning (cf. Schmitz 1968).
79 One could speak, with Heidegger and psychopathologist Kurt Schneider, of mineness.
80 See Blume (2003, 37-38).
81 Like pain, an emotion, and so forth.

reveal (*tua res agitur!*) that I am the one who is meant by the constant introduction of new descriptions as *explanantia* – that is, facts and qualities that, without this subjective nuance, are otherwise shared by many.

Luckily, the person as a conscious subject with the capability of self-ascription can always go back to this proto-identitary life (given as identical to us without identification and reflection thanks to "primitive present/presence"[82], in both a temporal and a spatial sense), by means of the vital drive and felt-bodily affective involvement – take the exemplary case, for Schmitz, of fright[83]. Self-ascription, by which identity is normally explained, is actually only possible (unless one wants to end up in a *regressus ad infinitum*) if it is based on self-consciousness without identification: that is, if I am already acquainted with myself[84]. Of course this primitive present/presence – as a guarantee of the coincidence between identity and subjectivity, and as a fusion point of five elements that cannot yet be distinguished (here, now, being, this and I) – at this point can and must also have a development[85]. What is later produced is an unfolded present/presence (the world): a condition that is emancipated (also by means of sentential speech) from life in the primitive present/presence, in which, as we have seen, all meanings are still subjective for someone.

As it explicates meanings by singularisation, the unfolded present/presence is differentiated in five polarities (here/space, now/time[86], being/not-being, this/relative identity, I/foreign). But Schmitz cares especially to highlight that the collapse of orientative dimensions made possible by this personal emancipation[87] – think of fright, but also real felt-

---

82 A real "mythogenous idea" (Stepath 2006, 119, 123). See also Griffero (2018b).

83 "Without receptivity to fright there would not be people who can take something as themselves" (Schmitz 2005a, 13). For one to be a felt body means that one can be cornered and scared (Schmitz 1989, 219).

84 The facts and qualities that are ascribed to me, for instance, can simply show who Tonino Griffero is, but not that I am indeed Tonino Griffero.

85 Also in an ontogenetic sense: for an application of this to child learning see Schultheis (1998, 93 sgg.).

86 For an analysis of time based on the critique of the unilateral development of the primitive present/presence in a relational temporality (instead of a more appropriate modal relational temporality) see Schmitz (1990, 247-274, and, more recently 2014c).

87 "People [...] do not simply present themselves as if they were new guests to a world already definitely divided into wholly individual things, but the very fact that they present themselves is an aspect of a fivefold structure of the primitive present/presence in a world endowed with its own form" (Schmitz 2003, 18).

bodily "catastrophes" like laughing and crying – is the only thing that, allowing the subject to regress to the primitive present/presence (personal regression), serves for personal re-subjectivisation. This regression implicates that the meanings are let fall back into their internally diffuse meaningfulness, thus certifying confidence with reality: a reality that, remember, in turn emerges only contextually to the emancipated subject – that is, only by the virtue of the abovementioned unfolding of the primitive present/presence[88].

From this original perspective, subjectivity is no longer the land to which to send into exile all that – by vagueness or complexity – falls under the reductionist razor, but rather the precise sphere of subjective situations for someone. In this sense, even "the word 'me' [is] to be understood not so much as a pronoun but rather as an adverb (a bit like 'here' and 'now'), one that does not denominate a thing but characterises a milieu, just as by the word 'here' one does not refer to a thing ('the here') but rather to what is here, in the immediate milieu" (Schmitz 1994a, 15). It follows that the person – albeit being a conscious subject with an ascribable content able to singularise and explicate the world (at first marked by internally and holistically diffuse meaningfulness) in the abovementioned five basic oppositions[89], – is alive and self-conscious, no matter what their "style" is[90], only if they have not completely emancipated themselves from (and can still access) the primitive present/presence. The unfolded present, in fact, is a labile stage and "fortunately" it's never acquired once and for all[91], so that the person[92] shows to be a chaotic and ambivalent phenomenon, infinitely (and therefore weakly) undecided about qualities like personality and prepersonality[93]. However, their substantial profile also always depends on their being unable to detach themselves from the subjective facts endowed with binding validity[94], and therefore also from atmospheric feelings.

---

88 "Reality appears all of a sudden, breaking the duration of subsisting in primitive present/presence (for example, when a sudden and intense noise wakes one up from dozing)" (Schmitz 2005a, 29).

89 Hence a latent hysteria in humans as such (Schmitz 1997, 173; see Stepath 2006, 124).

90 For example: pride, irony, stoic imperturbability, sober realism, etc. (Schmitz 1990, 155).

91 See Schmitz (2015, 119-137).

92 For a recent sumary see Schmitz (2017).

93 It is the logic of endless undecidness, to which Schmitz recurs several times (also in the text translated here) to avoid contradiction (see Blume 2003, 48-51). For this logical criterion, see Schmitz (2008, 115 ff.; 2013).

94 For binding validity in the culture of law and religion see Schmitz (1973, 1977, and, for a summary, 2012). For an interesting possible debate with Habermas'

5. *Conclusion.*

Now we can understand very well this summary mission statement, according to which New Phenomenology[95] should:

> allow self-contemplation to cast a – conceptually accurate – glance at the room for manoeuvre due to personal emancipation and personal regression between primitive present/presence and the unfolded present/presence; at the sentient felt body as a medium for every resonance and as a creative force endowed with specific spatiality and dynamics; at felt-bodily communication as the source of any contact in encorporation and excorporation; at felt-bodily and surfaceless spaces underlying the network formed by relative places; at feelings as gripping atmospheres; at situations in their different types and several stratifications, including especially rich impressions (impressive situations). [It has to] give back to human beings, thanks to understanding, the spontaneous life experience (Schmitz 2005a, 57).

Therefore, the point is to oppose the fatal intellectualistic paradigm of Western culture, certainly not thinking of radically revolutionizing the *status quo* or of disregarding completely, as early phenomenology would, the constraints of tradition – perhaps sacrificing in favour of archaic thought the undoubted advantages of "a lucid rationality that analyses, argues and criticises" (Schmitz 1999, 403). In other words, more realistically, the point is to suggest a healthy critical revision made possible by a heterodox philosophical "surfing"[96]. When reviving what has been repressed by the prevailing theoretical diktat, such surfing also takes the opportunity to "mock the strange illusion that it is always necessary to do something" (Schmitz 1965, 601).

In fact, New Phenomenology philosophically enhances not so much the activist-intellectual pride but rather the pride of those who are mature enough to be able to expose themselves profitably to the authority of the atmospheric feelings and collective situations of our spontaneous life experience. It speaks to those who can understand and appreciate also what

---

approach, starting from Schmitz's idea of unconditional seriousness and binding authority of feelings, see Lauterbach (2014).

95   Defined, with no false modesty, "the only attempt in the history of philosophy that managed to overcome the psychologistic-reductionist-introjectionist objectification (the source of the mistakes of dynamicism and autism), not only in theory but in practice" (Schmitz 1999, 403).

96   Schmitz (2005a, 107).

really happens to them in a felt manner, without them having intentionally constructed it; it speaks to those who do not postpone meaning and satisfaction to an unspecified and harmonistically conceived future, knowing, above all, that the primordial sphere (the world-matter according to Rothacker) necessarily transcends the finiteness of human descriptions[97]. Our will to live, in fact, should learn

> to anchor itself to the present through a tenuous balance, instead of evaporating into projections and projects become vacuous in the meantime. It should certainly strive for a better future and better living conditions, but not so that the agreement with the present life should need, like a crutch, a hope in something that is yet to come. Instead of this something, one should live the present/ presence (primitive e unfolded) with greater intensity, in the manner of those who are in love or dance, live their house or courageously exercise justice. Phenomenology cannot bring about this life form, but ensuring understanding of experience, it can prop up against collapses (as if it were the gallery of a mine) the depth of the present/presence in terms of a vision able to give an account of itself (Schmitz 2003, 19).

New Phenomenology defends (strict) subjectivity, the felt-bodily dimension and the emotional sphere (atmospheric and non-atmospheric) from the (today ubiquitous) cognitivist reductionism, thus giving back to the world its archaic "colour", defying the rationalist dogmatism that lives quietly in everyone of us – "how flat and boring would the world be without quasi-things!" (Schmitz 2003, 15). For these reasons, New Phenomenology is proving increasingly useful, as has been said, not only to philosophy but to many qualitative and interdisciplinary research paradigms.

And, in truth, the innovative power of this "new" approach is hampered neither by the strong polemical and anticonformist character of many of Schmitz's arguments, nor by their deliberate (philosophically healthy) one-sidedness and sharpness, even in conceptual and linguistic terms. What matters is that it does not leave us indifferent and deeply provokes our ordinary vision of things (objectification, dualism, introjection). To conclude, we could say that New Phenomenology mocks the (alleged) certainties of the intellectualist in the same way as in *Faust* Goethe ridicules the arrogant proktofantasmist[98].

---

97   Since there are many equivalent ways to fill the world, Schmitz (2014a, 131) calls himself a relativist at the epistemological level.

98   With a quote that is also dear to Schmitz (2003, 22).

Are you still here? This is unheard-of!
Vanish at one! This nonsense has been cleared up!
This devil-pack just won't observe the law.
We are so wise, yet ghosts can still haunt Tegel.
How long I've tried to clean away this folly!
But everything's still dirty. It's impossible![99]

Bibliography

Andermann, K./Eberlein, U. (eds.)
2011 *Gefühle als Atmosphären. Neue Phänomenologie und philosophische Emotionstheorie*, Akademie Verlag, Berlin.

Avenarius, R.
1912 *Der menschliche Weltbegriff,* introd. by Hermann Schmitz, ed. by R. Sohst, Xenomoi Verlag, Berlin 2014.

Becker, H. (ed.)
2013 *Zugang zu Menschen. Angewandte Philosophie in zehn Berufsfeldern*, Alber, Freiburg/München.

Blume, A.
2003 *Scham und Selbstbewusstsein. Zur Phänomenologie konkreter Subjektivität bei Hermann Schmitz*, Alber, Freiburg/München.
2010 *Hermann Schmitz (1928-)*, in: H. R. Sepp-L. Embree (eds.), *Handbook of Phenomenological Aesthetics*, Springer, Dordrecht et a., 307-309.

Böhme, G.
1989 *Für eine ökologische Naturästhetik*, Suhrkamp,Frankfurt a. M.
1995 *Atmosphäre. Essays zur neuen Ästhetik*, Suhrkamp, Frankfurt a. M.
1998 *Anmutungen. Über das Atmosphärische*, Tertium, Ostfildern v. Stuttgart.
2001 *Aisthetik. Vorlesungen über Ästhetik als allgemeine Wahrnehmungslehre*, Fink, München.
2006 *Architektur und Atmosphäre*, Fink, München.
2017a *The Aesthetics of Atmospheres*, Routledge, London-New York.
2017b *Atmospheric Architectures. The Aesthetics of Felt Spaces*, Bloomsbury, London et al.
2017c *Critique of Aesthetic Capitalism*, Mimesis International, Milan.

---

99   Vv. 4158-63 (Goethe 1949, 158).

Dörpinghaus, S.
2010 *Was Hebammen erspüren. Ein leiborientierter Ansatz in Theorie und Praxis*, Mabuse-Verlag, Frankfurt a. M.
2013 *Dem Gespür auf der Spur. Leibphänomenologische Studie zur Hebammenkunde am Beispiel der Unruhe*, Alber, Freiburg/München.

Fehige, J. H. Y.
2007 *Sexualphilosophie. Eine einführende Annäherung*, Lit, Berlin.

Fuchs, T.
2000 *Leib, Raum, Person. Entwurf einer phänomenologischen Anthropologie*, Klett-Cotta, Stuttgart.

Gahlings, U.
2006 *Phänomenologie der weiblichen Leiberfahrungen*, Alber, Freiburg/München.

Gamm, G.
1994 *Flucht aus der Kategorie*, Suhrkamp, Frankfurt a. M.

Goethe, J. W.
1949 *Faust*, Part I, by C. F. Mac Intyre, New Direction Books, New York
1998 *Maxims and Reflections*, tr. by E. Stopp, ed. by P. Hutchinson, Penguin Books, London et alia.

Griffero, T.
2013 *The atmospheric "skin" of the city*, "Ambiances. International Journal of Sensory Environment, Architecture and Urban Space", 1-19 http://ambiances.revues.org/399.
2014a *Atmospheres and Lived Space*, "Studia Phaenomenologica", 14 (Place, Environment, Atmosphere), 29-51.
2014b *Atmospheres. Aesthetics of Emotional Spaces*, Ashgate, Farnham.
2014c *Who's Afraid of Atmospheres (And of Their Authority)?*, "Lebenswelt", IV, 1, 193-213. http://riviste.unimi.it/index.php/Lebenswelt/article/view/4200
2014d *Architectural Affordances: The Atmospheric Authority of Spaces*, in: P. Tidwell (ed. by), *Architecture and Atmosphere*, Tapio Wirkkala-Rut Bryk Foundation, Espoo, 15-47.
2016a *Il pensiero del sensi. Atmosfere ed estetica patica*, Guerini & Associati, Milano.
2016b *Atmospheres and felt-bodily resonances*, "Studi di estetica", XLIV, 2016, 1, 1-41.
2016c Urbilder *o atmosfere?Ludwig Klages e la Nuova Fenomenologia*, "Annuario Filosofico", 32, 326-348
2016d *Felt-bodily communication: a neophenomenological approach to embodied affects* (Sensibilia 10-2016), "Studi di estetica", XLV, serie IV (8/2), 71-86.
2017a *Quasi-Things. The Paradigm of Atmospheres*, Suny Press, Albany.

2017b *Felt-Bodily Resonances. Towards a Pathic Aesthetics*, "Yearbook for Eastern and Western Philosophy" (Embodiment. Phenomenology East/West), 2, 149-164.
2018a *Something more. Atmospheres and pathic aesthetics*, in T. Griffero/G. Moretti (eds.), *Atmosphere/Atmospheres*, Mimesis International, Milan, 75-89.
2018b *Come Rain or Come Shine...The (Neo)Phenomenological Will-To-Presentness*, (Sensibilia 11-2017), "Studi di estetica", XLVI, serie IV (9/2), 57-73.

Grossheim, M.
1994 *Ludwig Klages und die Phänomenologie*, Akademie Verlag, Berlin

Großheim, M. (ed.)
1994 *Wege zu einer volleren Realität. Neue Phänomenologie in der Diskussion*, Akademie Verlag, Berlin.
2008 *Neue Phänomenologie zwischen Praxis und Theorie*, Alber, Freiburg.

Großheim, M./Kluck, S./Nörenberg, H.
2014 *Kollektive Lebensgefühle. Zur Phänomenologie von Gemeinschaften*, Rostocker Phænomenologische Manuskripte, 20.

Gugutzer, R.
2012 *Verkörperungen des Sozialen. Neophänomenologische Grundlagen und soziologische Analysen*, [transcript], Bielefeld.

Hasse, J.
2005 *Fundsachen der Sinne. Eine phänomenologische Revision alltäglichen Erlebens*, Alber, Freiburg/München.
2009 *Unbedachtes Wohnen. Lebensformen an verdeckten Rändern der Gesellschaft*, [transcript], Bielefeld.
2012 *Atmosphären der Stadt. Aufgespürte Räume*, jovis, Berlin.
2014 *Was Räume mit uns machen – und wir mit ihnen. Kritische Phänomenologie des Raumes*, Alber, Freiburg/München.
2015 *Der Leib der Stadt. Phänomenologische Annäherungen*, Alber, Freiburg/München.

Hasse, J. (ed.)
2008 *Die Stadt als Wohnraum*, Alber, Freiburg/München.

Hastedt, H.
1995 *Neuerscheinungen zum Leib-Seele-Problem*, "Philosophische Rundschau", 42, 254-263.

Hauskeller, M.
1995 *Atmosphären erleben. Philosophische Untersuchungen zur Sinneswahrnehmung*, Akademie Verlag, Berlin.

Hegel, G. W. F.
1821 *Philosophy of Right*, tr. by S. W. Dyde, Batoche Books Limited, Kitchener (Ontario) 2001.

Heubel, F.
2003 *Hermann Schmitz' Adolf Hitler in der Geschichte oder Zur Kritik der Neuen Phänomenologie*, in: T. Ogawa (ed.), *Studies on New Phenomenology and Theories of Collective Consciousness*, Graduate School of Global Environmental Studies, Kyoto, 41-51.

Julmi, C.
2015 *Atmosphären in Organisationen. Wie Gefühle das Zusammenleben in Organisationen beherrschen*, projektverlag, Bochum/Freiburg.
2017 *Situations and Atmospheres in Organizations. A (New) Phenomenology of Being-In-The-Organization*, Mimesis International, Milan.

Kammler, S.
2013 *Die Seele im Spiegel des Leibes. Der Mensch zwischen Leib, Seele und Körper bei Platon und in der Neuen Phänomenologie*, Alber, Freiburg/München.

Keller, F.
2013 *Eine kleine Einführung in die Neue Phänomenologie*, in: H. Becker (ed.), *Zugang zu Menschen. Angewandte Philosophie in zehn Berufsfeldern*, Alber, Freiburg/München, 227-246.

Kirchhoff, K.
2007 *Das gewisse Etwas. Phänomenologische Ansätze in der Religionspädagogik*, De Gruyter, Berlin.

Kluck, S.
2014 *Pathologien der Wirklichkeit. Ein phänomenologischer Beitrag zur Wahrnehmungstheorie und zur Ontologie der Lebenswelt*, Alber, Freiburg/München.
Kluck, S./Volke, S. (eds.)
2012 *Näher dran? Zur Phänomenologie des Wahrnehmens*, Alber, Freiburg/München.

Koll, J.
2007 *Körper beten. Religiöse Praxis und Körpererleben*, Kohlhammer, Stuttgart.

Landkammer, J.
*2000 Von Homer bis Hitler. Die "Neue Phänomenologie" und die Versuchung der Geschichtsphilosophie (*www.sicetnon.org/content/editormedien/schmitz.pdf*)*

Landweer, H.
2008 *Denken in Raumkategorien. Situation, Leib und Bedeutung bei Helmuth Plessner und Hermann Schmitz*, in: B. Accarino/M. Schloßberger (eds.), *Expres-*

sivität und Stil. Helmuth Plessners Sinnes- und Ausdruckphilosophie, Akademie Verlag, Berlin, 235-252.

Lauterbach, Sr. M. J.
2014 *"Gefühle mit der Autorität unbedingten Ernstes"*. *Eine Studie zur religiösen Erfahrung in Auseinandersetzung mit Jürgen Habermas und Hermann Schmitz*, Alber, Freiburg/München.

Linck, G.
2011 *Leib oder Körper. Mensch, Welt und Leben in der Chinesischen Philosophie*, Alber, Freiburg/München.

Moldzio, A.
2004 *Schizophrenie: eine philosophische Erkrankung*, Königshausen & Neumann, Würzburg.

Marcinski I
2014 *Anorexie – Phänomenologische Betrachtung einer Essstörung*, Alber, Freiburg/München.

Müller-Pelzer, W.
2012 *Interkulturelle Situationen – Verstrickung und Entfaltung. Die Perspektive der Neuen Phänomenologie*, Cuvillier Verlag, Göttingen.

Nörenberg, H.
2014 *Der Absolutismus des Anderen. Politische Theologien der Moderne*, Alber, Freiburg/München.

Preusker, J.
2014 *Die Gemeinsamkeit der Leiber. Eine sprachkritische Interexistenzialanalyse der Leibphänomenologie von Hermann Schmitz und Thomas Fuchs*, Lang, Frankfurt a. M.

Rappe, G.
1995 *Archaische Leiberfahrung. Der Leib in der frühgriechischen Philosophie und in außereuropäischen Kulturen*, Akademie Verlag, Berlin.
2012 *Leib und Subjekt. Phänomenologische Beiträge zu einem erweiterten Menschenbild*, projektverlag, Bochum/Freiburg.

Schmitz, H.
1957 *Hegel als Denker der Individualität*, Hain, Meisenheim.
1959 *Goethes Altersdenken im problemgeschichtlichen Zusammenhang*, Bouvier, Bonn.
1964 *System der Philosophie*, I: Die Gegenwart, Bouvier, Bonn.
1965 *System der Philosophie*, II: 1. Teil: Der Leib, Bouvier, Bonn.

1966 *System der Philosophie*, II: 2. Teil: Der Leib im Spiegel der Kunst, Bouvier, Bonn

1967 *System der Philosophie*, III: Der Raum, 1. Teil: Der leibliche Raum, Bouvier, Bonn.

1968 *Subjektivität. Beiträge zur Phänomenologie und Logik*, Bouvier, Bonn.

1969 *System der Philosophie*, III: Der Raum, 2. Teil: Der Gefühlsraum, Bouvier, Bonn.

1972 *Nihilismus als Schicksal?*, Bouvier, Bonn.

1973 *System der Philosophie*, III: Der Raum, 3. Teil: Der Rechtsraum, Bouvier, Bonn.

1977 *System der Philosophie*, III: Der Raum, 4. Teil: Das Göttliche und der Raum, Bouvier, Bonn.

1978 *System der Philosophie*, III: Der Raum, 5. Teil: Die Wahrnehmung, Bouvier, Bonn.

1980a *System der Philosophie*, IV: Die Person, Bouvier, Bonn.

1980b *System der Philosophie*, V: Die Aufhebung der Gegenwart, Bouvier, Bonn

1980c *Neue Phänomenologie*, Bouvier, Bonn.

1985a *Phänomenologie der Leiblichkeit*, in: H. Petzold (ed.), *Leiblichkeit. Philosophische, gesellschaftliche undtherapeutische Perspektiven*, Junfermann, Paderborn, 71-106.

1985b *Die Ideenlehre des Aristoteles*, I: Aristoteles 1 Teil: Kommentar zum 7. Buch der Metaphysik; Die Ideenlehre des Aritoteles, 1: Aristoteles, 2 Teil: Ontologie, Noologie, Theologie; Die Ideenlehre des Aritoteles, 2: Platon und Aristoteles, Bouvier, Bonn.

1988a *Anaximander und die Anfänge der griechischen Philosophie*, Bouvier, Bonn.

1988b *Der Ursprung des Gegenstandes. Von Parmenides bis Demokrit*, Bouvier, Bonn.

1990 *Der unerschöpfliche Gegenstand. Grundzüge der Philosophie*, Bouvier, Bonn 1990 (2007[3]).

1992 *Leib und Gefühl. Materialien zu einer philosophischen Therapeutik*, Junfermann, Paderborn.

1993 *Die Liebe*, Bouvier, Bonn 2007[2].

1994a *Wozu Neue Phänomenologie?*, in: M. Großheim (ed.), *Wege zu einer volleren Realität. Neue Phänomenologie in der Diskussion*, Akademie Verlag, Berlin, 7-18.

1994b *Neue Grundlagen der Erkenntnistheorie*, Bouvier, Bonn.

1996 *Husserl und Heidegger*, Bouvier, Bonn.

1997 *Höhlengänge. Über die gegenwärtige Aufgabe der Philosophie*, Akademie Verlag, Berlin.

1999a *Adolf Hitler in der Geschichte*, Bouvier, Bonn.

1999b *Der Spielraum der Gegenwart*, Bouvier, Bonn.

2002 *Begriffene Erfahrung. Beiträge zur antireduktionistischen Phänomenologie*, with G. Marx e A. Moldzio, Koch Verlag, Rostock.

2003 *Was ist Neue Phänomenologie?*, Koch Verlag, Rostock.

2005a with W. Sohst, *Im Dialog. Neun neugierige und kritische Fragen an die Neue Phänomenologie*, Xenomoi, Berlin.

2005b *Was ist ein Phänomen?*, in: D. Schmoll/A. Kuhlmann (eds.), *Symptom und Phänomen. Phänomenologische Zugänge zum kranken Menschen*, Alber, Freiburg/München, 16-28.

2005c *Situationen und Konstellationen. Wider die Ideologie totaler Vernetzung*, Alber, Freiburg/München.

2007 *Der Leib, der Raum und die Gefühle*, Edition Sirius, Bielefeld-Locarno.

2008 *Logische Untersuchungen*, Alber, Freiburg/München

2009a *Die Neue Phänomenologie. Ein Gespräch mit Hermann Schmitz* (Andreas Brenner), "Information Philosophie", 5, Dezember, 20-29.

2009b *Kurze Einführung in die Neue Phänomenologie*, Alber, Freiburg/München.

2010a *Jenseits des Naturalismus*, Alber, Freiburg/München.

2010b *Bewusstsein*, Alber, Freiburg/München

2011 *Der Leib*, De Gruyter, Berlin/Boston.

2012 *Das Reich der Normen*, Alber, Freiburg/München.

2013 *Kritische Grundlegung der Mathematik. Eine phänomenologisch-logische Analyse*, Alber, Freiburg/München.

2014a *Gibt es die Welt?*, Alber, Freiburg/München.

2014b *Atmosphären*, Alber, Freiburg/München.

2014c *Phänomenologie der Zeit*, Alber, Freiburg/München.

2015 *selbst sein. Über Identität, Subjektivität und Personalität*, Alber, Freiburg/München.

2016 *Ausgrabungen zum wirklichen Leben. Eine Bilanz*, Alber, Freiburg/München.

2017 *Zur Epigenese der Person*, Alber, Freiburg/München.

2018 *Wozu philosophieren?*, Alber, Freiburg/München.

Schmoll, D./Kuhlmann A. (eds.)
2005 *Symptom und Phänomen. Phänomenologische Zugänge zum kranken Menschen*, Alber, Freiburg/München.

Schultheis, K.
1998 *Leiblichkeit – Kultur – Erziehung. Zur Theorie der elementaren Erziehung*, Deutscher Studien Verlag, Weinheim.

Soentgen, J.
1998 *Die verdeckte Wirklichkeit. Einführung in die Neue Phänomenologie von Hermann Schmitz*, Bouvier, Bonn.

Stepath, K.
2006 *Gegenwartskonzepte. Eine philosophisch-literaturwissenschhaftliche Analyse temporaler Strukturen*, Köenigshausen & Neumann, Würzburg.

Thomas, P.
1996 *Selbst-Natur-Sein. Leibphänomenolgie als Naturphilosophie*, Akademie Verlag, Berlin.

Uzarewicz, C./Uzarewicz, M.
2005 *Das Weite suchen. Einführung in eine phänomenologische Anthropologie für Pflege*, Lucius und Lucius, Stuttgart.

Uzarewicz, M.
2011 *Der Leib und die Grenzen der Gesellschaft. Eine neophänomenologische Soziologie des Transhumanen*, Lucius und Lucius, Stuttgart.

Volke, S.
2007 *Sprach-physiognomik. Grundlagen einer leibphänomenologischen Beschreibung der Lautwahrnehmung*, Alber, Freiburg/München.

Werhahn, H.
2003 *Die Neue Phänomenologie und ihre Themen*, Koch Verlag, Rostock.
Werhahn. H. (ed.)

2011 *Neue Phänomenologie. Hermann Schmitz im Gespräch*, Alber, Freiburg/München.

Wolf, B.
2012 *Bildung und Sozialisation in der frühen Kindheit. Eine qualitative Studie unter Einbeziehung von Richard Sennetts Flexibilitätskonzept und Hermann Schmitz' Neuer Phänomenologie*, Alber, Freiburg/München.

New Phenomenology, as I have conceived and developed it, aims to make their actual lives comprehensible to humans, that is, to make accessible again spontaneous life experience in continuous contemplation after having cleared away artificial ideas prefigured in history. Spontaneous life experience is anything that happens to humans in a felt manner without their having intentionally constructed it. Today, human thought is so enthralled by seemingly natural assumptions of conventions and hypotheses in the service of constructions that it has become painstaking to disclose spontaneous life experience; but doing so is of great importance, because it can point the way out of dangerous limitations and entanglements of the human understanding of self and world and, in consequence, aid in finding a better way of living.

So far, an introduction that gives a coherent overview of the central ideas of New Phenomenology has been missing. My book *Was ist Neue Phänomenologie?* [What is New Phenomenology?], published in 2003 in Rostock, was not intended as an introduction, but as an overview. Grouped around a collection of central issues, it offers a series of essays based on talks I gave. To my surprise it was considered to be difficult even by kind and well-informed readers. It is my hope that the present book lends itself better to being read smoothly. But I do want to point out that it is no mere first jab, but a proper introduction to New Phenomenology. Thus, it does not offer tasty bites but rather coherent trains of thought which are properly developed. In so doing, I try to take the reader by the hand. For this reason, I subdivided the contents into seven hours, so that the reader may get into the overarching train of thought.

This text is an elaboration of six talks delivered at the educational institution "Bildungshaus Stella Matutina" of the sisterhood of Baldegger at the Vierwaldstätter Lake. Indeed, I am very grateful for the extraordinarily friendly and understanding reception in that wonderful environment. Without this event, this book would not have come to be. May it stand as a monument in memory of the wonderful days spent there!

I
First Hour
Why Philosophy? Philosophy and Science. The Phenomenological
Method: What Is the Aim of New Phenomenology?

The conception of New Phenomenology originates from my idea
of philosophy. Over the course of history, two intertwining ways of
interpreting it have been competing with one another:

1. Philosophy as the speculative construction of the universe (from
Anaximander to the metaphysical systems of Spinoza, Leibniz and Hegel):
this project was attractive as long as not too much complicated and
specialised knowledge, often becoming obsolete all too fast, had accrued
in the sciences. Today, a speculatively constructing philosopher would be
a Quixotic figure. The courage for such adventures has, in the meantime,
been taken over by the specialised sciences. Physicists no longer speculate
about the universe, but about a multiverse of many universes.

2. Philosophy as introspective contemplation: already Heraclitus
wrote: "I have explored myself." But isolated contemplation in solitude
is not sufficient for philosophy. For this reason, I have adopted the
following definition and have often advanced it since 1964: *philosophy
is man's contemplation of how he finds himself in his environment.*
The motivation for doing this is an irritation of this process of finding
oneself. Everyone who is not entirely certain of their embeddedness and
tries to give themselves an account of this uncertainty philosophises in
this manner. This cannot always be backed up scientifically, because
there is not as much time to give such accounts as science would need.
As soon as the person philosophising brings their contemplation into
conversation, questions arise: how do you mean this? How do you know
that? The first question leads to a definition, the second to an explanation.
Thus, philosophical contemplation is on its way to becoming science.
But philosophy can also become supraindividually important as a non-
scientific philosophy if a human's contemplation of their finding themself
in their environment becomes exemplary for other's understanding of
self and world. Great non-scientific philosophers have been, for instance,
Heraclitus, Kierkegaard and Nietzsche.

I now turn to the relation of philosophy to the 'regular' (extra-philosophical) sciences. Regular sciences aim to discover objective facts to solve objective problems. Philosophy aims to find objective facts to solve subjective problems. I use the expressions 'subjective' and 'objective' in an unusual manner, i.e. as epithets not for subjects and objects but for meanings, which include states of affairs, programs and problems. Such a meaning is objective if everyone can say it (not merely name it), insofar as they know enough and are sufficiently articulate; it is subjective if one person at the most can say it (using their own name); this is the case if they afflict them, if their affective involvement hangs on them. This distinction is of crucial importance to my thinking; I return to it in section (III). For now, I merely want to illustrate it with an example of programs and problems. For officers, before and during a battle, which can also be a democratic electoral campaign, the battle plan is a wish (understood as a program, not as a state of the soul, i.e. a mental state) and, if the battle reaches a critical stage, a worry (as a problem). Everyone has their own wishes, their own worries, which no one else can articulate because of the highly personal involvement that has gone into this meaning. Language expresses this by use of the ethical dative case in German, for instance, if a mother says "Möge er mir unversehrt bleiblen." [lit.trans. "May he remain unharmed to me."]. Thus, desire and worry are subjective meanings in the sense specified here. For a historian, soberly registering historical facts, this subjectivity is irrelevant; instead of being a wish for them, the battle plan is merely an objective program. In recounting the critical stage of the battle, it poses merely an objective problem for him.

I now mention examples of such philosophical, i.e. subjective problems. Amongst them can be counted Kant's three questions: what can I know? What ought I to do? What may I hope? Further such questions are, for example: What concerns me? What should I really take seriously? What can I overlook? What will I overlook if I let myself be guided? What am I capable of? (this question is the source of the problem of freedom) From where do I get the courage to continue living despite death, guilt and suffering? Who am I, as myself, beyond what is done to me? What is singular, am I singular? Am I the same person as someone who once lived or as someone who is yet to be? If I believe that I am something, what does the fact that *I* am it consist in? How can I be a whole? What is real about me? What does it mean to say that something is real? Sciences and other sources want to teach me facts; but what does it mean to be a fact?

Such questions get their subjectivity for the person philosophizing from the irritation of their attempts to find themselves in their environment.

All these questions and many other subjective problems can be summed up in the question: what should I take to hold true? This is the fundamental question of philosophy, as it is the central question of phenomenology. In addressing this question, the proposed method is that of phenomenological revision, in order to turn as much obscure belief as possible into determinate assumptions and test them on the following question: of which suggested state of affairs can I not seriously (in good conscience) deny that it is a fact? What stands up to this test then, to me, is a phenomenon. So the definition of a phenomenon in the sense of New Phenomenology runs as follows: *a phenomenon for someone at a time is a state of affairs of which the person cannot in earnest deny that it then is a fact.* In contrast to the notion of 'phenomenon' propounded by older phenomenologists (e.g. Husserl, Scheler, Heidegger), it has two distinctive features:

1. The double relativisation to someone and to the particular point in time of each phenomenological revision. New Phenomenology no longer wants to lay claim to establishing something with apodictic certainty for all eternity. That is merely a regulative principle guided by the good faith that there still is a point in hoping for agreement with others in selecting phenomena. The phenomenologist may never give up this good faith, since he needs to remain focused on a comparison of his own beliefs with those of others in expectancy of possible agreement in order not to limit his field of vision and thus the scope of phenomenological revision. At any rate, he can never be sure he has exhausted this scope; maybe some possibilities of reconsideration, according to which the claim to being a phenomenon should have been measured, never occurred to him. By double relativisation, phenomenology becomes a thoroughly empirical endeavour/science in the context of which one has to constantly re-examine whether something is still a phenomenon for one.

2. Traditional phenomenology chooses as phenomena "what is revealed" (Heidegger), the "things themselves" (Husserl). But a thing only comes into being in a perspective, in the light of the language used and in the historically pre-figured points of view or aspects, under which something can be understood as an instance of something. In itself, what is revealed is ambiguous because it can be put in relation to many perspectives. States of affairs, however, also contain the aspect of the thing by determining something as a case of something. For this reason, the concept of a state of affairs is to be preferred to the concept of a thing in describing phenomena.

Phenomenological revision serves to approximate the spontaneous life experience, i.e. what really happens to people in a felt manner without them having intentionally constructed it. Spontaneous life experience is the ultimate yardstick for the justification of assertions; any other justification is based on constructions and, as such, can be called into doubt. But spontaneous life experience is not a safe harbour that can be easily sailed into; rather, it is only accessible through a filter of pre-figured perspectives (on the basis of abstraction). Phenomenology as a research endeavour is unique in that it tends to choose a basis of abstraction for concept formation that is closer to spontaneous life experience, in that it delves more deeply into it and seeks to fathom its richness and originality. This tendency runs counter and is complementary to the tendency of science, as aimed at schematic prognosis, in the interest of which spontaneous life experience is ground down to a few types of features ideally suited to experiments and statistics and which are used to check theoretical prognoses.

Natural science can experimentally check the expectations generated by its theories, and while it cannot determine their correctness, it can assess their prognostic value. Such an intersubjectively unquestionable yardstick is not available for phenomenology; it can only call on the evidence of the moment (Manfred Sommer), which makes it impossible for a phenomenologist to doubt a phenomenon because it asserts itself as fact in the face of all conceivable variations of assumptions. This double dependence on the phenomenologist and the moment gives rise to sceptical questions of how claim can be laid to the intersubjective validity of the results of phenomenological research and how this research can make progress. The latter question is easily answered: progress consists in determining, in ever more detail, what is salient. Phenomenology is a learning process of refining one's attention and expanding one's horizon for possible assumptions. Only by invitation to participate in this learning process can the phenomenologist attempt to convince his audience. In so doing, he is not restricted to merely assuring that he has found this or that phenomenon. Much rather, in a state of affair presenting itself as a fact, he can find nuances that, if pondered in detail, unavoidably give cause to draw inferences that have results incompatible with certain beliefs. Thus, the way has been cleared for argumentative discourse and intersubjectively possible clarification beyond mere assertion. Of course, one cannot reach an agreement with people that are already dead, since one cannot talk to them. But the phenomenological gap to their positions is bridged by the reasonable assumption of mostly similar experience. It is quite likely that Goethe did not have ten legs but, like us, only two. It is equally likely that he will have occasionally been angry or fearful, spoken German, got up from a chair, chewed solid food etc. Of course, all this could, in principle, have been experienced very differently by him than by us – e.g. getting up out of the chair as fainting or rapture. But this could hardly be taken seriously. So our exact focus on our spontaneous life experience will ordinarily yield results that can, for the most part, be applied to Goethe. Differences in individual or cultural formation are, of course, to be expected. But they can be taken into account if one introduces concept formation at a high level of abstraction and, by trying out specific differences, adjusts it to the available testimony of different life forms. In so doing, it is important to place the other and oneself in the specifically relevant historical context. It is often sufficient to explain sedimentations in the understanding of self and world that complicate finding congruence in the phenomena. It can also make accessible experiences that the phenomenologist was not yet familiar with and that henceforth expand the playing field of his phenomenological revision.

In its empirical humbleness of following up on spontaneous life experience instead of wanting to apodictically deliver ultimate justifications by means of transcendental speculation or contemplating essences, New Phenomenology is marked by an openness which other branches of philosophy lack: its utility in the context of applied sciences. Here, two needs are particularly effective. Some sciences are under a lot of pressure from the experimental and statistical methods of natural science, and their empirical findings need to be phenomenologically complemented, since their methods do away with too much; others are not suitable to being scientifically scrutinised but need to be more firmly rooted, which New Phenomenology can do. In brackets I provide examples for both groups how New Phenomenology has inspired other disciplines. We should, however, keep in mind that it has not yet had as much influence as it could and should have. Group one: architecture (theory of dwelling, interior spaces, urban environments), geography (designed spaces), medicine (chronic conditions, e.g. diabetes; orthopaedics), phonetics (conversations as embodied communication), psychiatry and psychotherapy (disorders of personality and embodiment, e.g. schizophrenia). Second group: pedagogy (situations and atmospheres in education, e.g. class rooms), nursing (the felt body, embodied communication, emotions as atmospheres), sinology (the Chinese view of man), applied theology. Another potential field of application of New Phenomenology not yet dealt with lies in the realm of law, to which it would bring and elaborate philosophy of law based on the authority of emotions in relevant situations; from here, important hints for understanding politics could be taken. The theory of embodied relatedness of figures by embodied bridging qualities (suggestion of motion and synaesthetic characters) has appealed to many artists. As regards the applicability of New Phenomenology to applied sciences and living practices, I was surprised to stumble across an article by Tanja Bossmann on phenomenology in the in the "Zeitschrift für Physiotherapeuten" [Journal for Physiotherapists] 60, 2008, p. 984:

> For medicine and psychology, New Phenomenology, introduced by Herrmann Schmitz in the 1960s, is particularly relevant (...) In contrast to other philosophical approaches, New Phenomenology is fundamentally oriented towards experience and applicability. Thus, it is possible to maintain an openness to reality and, at the same time, a thorough scepticism towards premature conclusions. In this sense, New Phenomenology wants to part with the schematisations of science and disclose new opportunities for experience.

Phenomenology is a fairly young field of research that directs philosophical attention to making explicit and testing what indubitably is the case (even before a belief has been formed). Maybe we can see it as already taking shape in Locke's *Essay Concerning Human Understanding*. At this stage, however, it is still deeply mired in scientistic and theological prejudice, from which it is freed only by Hume's scepticism, in which we may see the first buds of a genuinely phenomenological growth. As a basic philosophical stance, it is proclaimed by Husserl, whose ideal of an open phenomenological perspective, however, is obstructed by the seeming naturalness of the metaphysical tradition and a mathematical thought style; Heidegger introduces a few expansions but gets stuck in the first steps. For such reasons, New Phenomenology must yet again attempt to uncover spontaneous life experience, which has been lost from sight of a thought style primarily interested in constructions. In so doing, however, it cannot do away with all constructions. Its uniqueness consists in the task to which these constructions are put. Thus it counteracts distractions from spontaneous life experience, which have three main sources: 1. Philosophy, mainly classical, 2. Theology, mainly late classical and medieval, 3. Natural science, beginning in the early modern period (since 1600). To this is added the suggestive force of naturally grown language, which draws on all three sources. Mankind is helplessly carried away with technological progress and social connectedness by an unavoidable amount of offers without having salient conceptual criteria for self-contemplation and thus asserting itself. New Phenomenology aims to aid humans by equipping them with poignant but elegant concepts that enable involved self-contemplation. How important this task is only becomes clear in retrospectively looking back at the European history of man's understanding of self and world. For this reason, I now turn to a brief overview of this topic.

The Historical Prefigurations of the Human
Understanding of Self and World in Europe

Spontaneous life experience can only be uncovered if its distortions by historical shaping, which have become fossilised as truisms in the day to day consciousness of contemporary man, are re-examined and then dislodged.

These cultural templates are predated by the self-understanding of the figures of Homer's *Iliad*. Contemporary man construes his experience as centred on a private inner sphere that is closed off to the outside world and in which reason is considered the centre of the governance of spontaneous impulses. The figures of the *Iliad*, as the poet portrays them, construe their experience differently: without being the master in their own private sphere (a soul), they are part of a concert of semi-autonomous sources of impulse, which partly drive, inhibit or control in a manner similar to the way conscience drives us; it is a comparable remaining source of impulse, one, however, which is not localised in the felt body. They are exposed to obsession by gods or affects. Ares takes hold of Hector just as rage does of Achilles. Therefore, they are exposed to upheavals that are difficult to contain. In contrast, a tendency towards self-control gains prevalence in the *Odyssey*, which can be seen in three differences to the *Iliad,* exemplified by Odysseus: first, he distances himself from his embodied impulses by complaining about his hunger, which drives him to eat, whereas he would rather mourn having been separated from home. He tames his violent heart by benevolent coaxing like a master tames his dogs; second, without obsession, he faces the gods as a reliable ally or opponent; third, he is able to exert complete control over his facial expression.

Only in the wake of this Homeric tendency toward self-empowerment, partly many centuries afterwards, does the Psyché – originally life as quality and not as life-time – develop into a soul as a private inner sphere in which the experience of the conscious subject is enclosed. In the case of Heraclitus in the early 5th century BC it is not yet this closed off; one of his aphorisms runs: "Of soul thou shalt never find boundaries, not if thou trackest it on every path"[1]. In archaic lyric poetry (7th and 6th century BC) and in the tragedian Aeschylus (first half of the 5th century BC), just as in the *Iliad*, the passivity of embodied drivenness by gods and affects dominates, even though the subject occasionally sets itself off by "But I". The tragedian Sophocles (second half of the 5th century BC) characterises the experience of his characters: the Sophoclean man can manipulate his emotions, for instance, contain his anger, work himself up into a state of grief, let what is uplifting or depressing grow. Here the soul becomes a closed off inner sphere with a gate that can also be opened; furthermore, as a source of impulse, it is the person's partner who speaks with him. What is new in Sophocles, as well as in his contemporary Herodotus, are phrases such as "to get out of oneself" and "to be beside oneself". They indicate that the person is identified with an inner sphere, as though it jumped out of itself, when it leaves this sphere. Up to this time, the golden Aphrodite exemplified the erotic, in which merely the lyric poet Mimnermus (7th century BC) wished to live as in the sun, fearful of old age, when Aphrodite's gold no longer shines; Pindar (first half of the 5th century BC) still speaks of a young girl that, when seduced by Apollo, first touches the sweet Aphrodite. After the break in human self-understanding, from 450 BC onwards, the erotic changes from an atmosphere into private pleasure. Aristophanes' Lysistrata silences the danger of the men breaking the sexual strike intended to end the Peloponnesian war with the argument: "There is no joy in it."

At the same time as human self-understanding is transformed, so is the understanding of the world; the watershed for this development lies in the second half of the 5th century BC between Empedocles and Democritus. Up to that point, the philosophers' understanding of the world is determined by meaningful impressions that are read off of the poles of dual forces. In the case of Anaximenes there is the tautened and the lax, in the case of Parmenides, the cumbersomely bulky in contrast to the light and quick; they are associated with the masculine and the feminine and, correspondingly, with the contrast between the two worldly forces of conflict (anger) and love according to Empedocles. The polar sequence of the Pythagoreans is less favourable towards the feminine. They place the border, the one, the just, the masculine, the calm, the straight, the good, the square and

---

1   Quoted from Diogenes Laertius (1925, book IX, chapter 1, 7).

the light on the one side and, on the other side, the infinite, the many, the left, the feminine, the movable, the bent, the bad, the dark and the scalene rectangle. The dynamism of these forces, the interaction of which Heraclitus illustrates using the bow metaphor, in the case of Leucippus and Democritus, becomes the mere kinetics of whirling atoms; in the course of the 5th century, Heraclitus' law of the conflict of opposites becomes the trivial pseudo-Heraclitean slogan: "Everything flows." This flow of muddled kinetics is balanced by contrasting it with stable invariants: Democritus' atoms (which he calls "ideas"), Platonic-Aristotelian ideas, laws of nature in Modernity. These invariants determine the shape of the sensuous material. Thinking in terms of matter and form already begins as early as Democritus (in the image of the shaping of man) and, in Plato and Aristotle, becomes a motif that foreshadows a technical orientation. According to this schema, man is divided into body and soul. Here the body functions as material and servant, while the soul is its shaping force and helmsman. The soul becomes a closed-off inner sphere with an enclosed mind, which can only be accessed from the outside through the five senses. With the exception of a few standard types of features, i.e. unspecific sense qualities (size, shape, number, motion, position, order), and their posited carriers (atoms), the external world is ground down. The remainder of this grinding down is, quite literally, disposed of in the soul or ignored and then furtively dragged along in it.

On the pro side, this *psychologistic-reductionist-introjectionist objectification* provides ample opportunities for taking hold of the self and the world. By being given a soul, man receives a house for his experience, in which he can and should be master over spontaneous impulses; thus the problem of emotional upheaval encountered by the characters in the *Iliad* is resolved. The types of qualities left in the external world by Democritus (and Plato in his *Timaeus*) are ideally suited to statistics and experiments because of intermomentary and intersubjective identifiability, measurement and selective variability; for this reason today they still provide the entire corpus of data which is used in physics to test the validity and predictive power of hypotheses deduced from theories and ultimately to test the theories themselves. This pro side stands in contrast to the con side that the most important contents of spontaneous life experience are repressed or forgotten: the felt body – which would seem to have fallen through in between the (material) body and the soul – and embodied communication (in exchanging glances and several other occasions in daily life), emotions as atmospheres, significant situations and, amongst them, rich impressions, the surfaceless spaces (passed over by Greek Geometry) of weather, sound, posture, felt impulses, emotion etc.; also half-things: voice, wind, an overpowering sense of gravity, pain as an imposing opponent and not merely as a state of the soul, emotions as half-things moving the felt body.

In the wake of the psychologistic-reductionist-introjectionist objectification, philosophers become advocates for and agents of self- and world-empowerment; in antiquity this is still restricted to self-empowerment by governance over spontaneous impulses, the main topic of the post-Democritean schools of philosophy, with the exception of the heathen Neo-Platonism of late antiquity. Since the rise of Christianity, world-empowerment is the prerogative of God the Almighty, whose overseeing of eternal salvation or damnation, by means of the fear of sin, at the same time enhances self-empowerment to become folk-discipline. Christianity's strongest educational influence on mankind lies in tying affective involvement to the topic of power. All other topics of affective involvement, such as honour and reputation, family and friendship, love, lust, suffering, aging, sickness and death are subordinated to the topic of power, namely the power of God over the individual's future good or ill fortune. Thus a boost towards modernity is triggered. The most important Church Father of the late Antiques, Augustine, as early as then is a mostly modern man, since he ties the purely technical attitude of a dispassionate user of earthly objects to the only goal of one's own happiness and sees his own body as merely a machine that ruins his sex life by not entirely submitting to his will. What is not modern about Augustine is that he seeks happiness as eternal blessedness in submission to God and uniformity in the community of the Church (as well as, in the case of success, among the Blessed in Heaven).

In medieval Christianity the passive relationship to power as the dominant topic of affective involvement soon takes on active features, because humans (the Pope, the clergy), according to the contemporary view, have power delegated by God and, in their name, others can also exact military power (e.g. Crusaders). Abusing it for worldly purposes – e.g. the 4th Crusade redirected to Constantinople by the Pope in his function as worldly ruler for the purpose of pillaging – strips this power of its transcendence and brings it eye-to-eye with worldly power. This process is completed around 1300. Philipp the Fair is the first worldly ruler who no longer takes the transcendent nimbus of the Papacy seriously and thus asserts himself against the Pope, who is intimidated and relocates to

Avignon in the King's sphere of influence. This has the consequence that the Church is divided for a long time, since there soon is a new Pope in Rome. From then on, man can take power, as the dominant theme of his affective involvement, into his own hands.

At the same time, a further precondition for this emerges. The singularism – the conviction that everything is singular – which has long since been latently guiding Scholasticism, is radically formulated by William of Ockham with historical weight: every entity, even every accidens, every property is an entity onto itself (ens a se) that exists by itself, independent of everything else; there are no relations, not even a unifying world order encompassing all particulars. Based on this is Constellationism, an understanding of the world as a network of individual factors. A network can be re-arranged; thus, with Ramon Llull, a passion for constructing combinatorial systems takes hold and ultimately leads to Leibniz's project of a Characteristica Universalis, which has the aim of making all problem solutions calculable by universal combinatorics and in the insuperable maximisation of combinability through the conception of all possible worlds. But the re-arrangement of networks is also the general mode of working in modern technology; it is already sketched in Ockham's redefinition of technical manufacture, which had been characterised by Aristotle as the realisation of a programme internal to the technician's mind: for Ockham it is the re-arrangement of pieces in space; thus, the way is paved for trying out, tinkering and re-combining networks.

As early as around 1300, the time would have been right for Bacon and Hobbes; it is only a small step from Ockham to them. Rather, it takes three centuries until man empowers himself to take the power into the hands of his own technical ability. This is partly rooted in the resurgence of pre-Democritean archaic imagistic thinking as Magia Naturalis in the dusk of medieval Christianity (15th/16th century). Here we have the second renaissance of archaic thinking since the Apostolic Age. The early Christian mentality under the auspices of the Holy Spirit – a feeling of love, joy and openness (Parrhesia), in which the early Christians lived together in the expectation of Christ's imminent return – places them on the same level of human self-understanding as Aeschylus and Empedocles. St. Paul's man, as felt body, stands in the tension between the moving but conflicting atmospheric forces of mind and flesh, which behave like love and strife according to Empedocles, i.e. not in a Platonic sense of an opposition between the mental and the sensuous. According to the First

Epistle of John, absolute love expurgates fear, which is to be understood literally. Later, Christianity adopted the psychologistic-reductionist-introjectionist objectification and replaced archaic thinking with it. Because of this unworldly attitude, reductionism of the external world took a step back without disappearing. Christianity has expanded the potential for empowerment contained in this objectification: self-empowerment was promoted to the point of isolating individuals (connected to uniformity in the church) by worries about the salvation of one's individual soul and cautious control of spontaneous impulses in obedience to God; world-empowerment was prepared by tying affective involvement to the topic of power. In the Modern Era, Christianity's dominance is taken over by the Enlightenment. It takes over Christianity's Eudaimonia, makes it worldly and combines it with technical world-empowerment: everyone is entitled to use the powerful tools of modern technology. Thus results the alliance of modern Enlightenment with private capitalism, which is realised in Voltaire. It's Augustine's position, only that transcendence plays no role.

Natural scientific singularist thinking objectifies and particularises everything that can be experienced, including man's self-experience. Hume takes himself to be merely a bundle of perceptions. There is, however, nothing about them that would indicate that they are tied to me. Where am I in such a world of neutral elements? The philosopher who poses this question is Johann Gottlieb Fichte. Thus, he approximates the discovery of subjective facts (III) but misses them and encapsulates the self in an action that only performs itself. Since he cannot maintain this isolation, he sacrifices it to the compromise of (the faculty of) productive imagination that floats among and above all facts in the conflict between dependence and independence. By Friedrich Schlegel this is turned into romantic irony as the capacity to withdraw from any point of view and therefore also to take any such. In so doing he initiates the Age of Ironism that lasts to this very day. The downside of irony is fear as the vertigo of floating above one's possibilities (Kierkegaard). In the 19th century, floating ironically required an effort; thus the (literary and lived) figure of the dandy developed, marked by a feeling of homelessness and "Weltschmerz" [world-weariness]. The dandy wears masks under which he cannot be found; in apathy he maintains a skilfully enacted stance of disinterestedness on the fringes of the turmoil of human affairs, not with the composure of the stoic, but to protect himself against a fall that would bind him. From this position on the fringes he jumps to an immediate provocation from which he erratically retreats. This effort of maintaining an ironically floating position is no longer required of an ironist in the 20th century and after. His ironic stance has become passive and folkish. He is cool. While the Christian's striving was strictly regimented by an ideal of happiness and salvation (especially as military service for Christ in Calvinism) and this regimentation showed after-effects in the age of Enlightenment, in the Ironist Age man confronts the innumerable affordances of technical possibilities, which take hold of him if he engages in them. Amongst one another, they are connected in a constellationist network; but for him, they are isolated and spread out. He brings no backbone, no direction, to navigating the spread-out affordances, since he is ironistically prepared to be able to turn away from anything and to anything. His ironism has slackened and become the passivity of self-absorption in the guidance by networked affordances with the seeming sovereignty of being able to freely choose among them.

III
THIRD HOUR

The Person and the Pre-Personal Foundations of Self-Consciousness;
Affective Involvement; Subjective vs. Objective Facts; the Primitive
Present; Embodied Dynamism; Embodied Communication; Identity
Without Singularity; the Felt Body Without a Soul

In my view, a person is a conscious subject with the ability of self-ascription. Self-ascription consists in taking something to be oneself (or oneself to be something). All specific personal performances arise from this ability: taking responsibility, giving an account of oneself, allotting oneself a place in the environment of people, things and states of affairs. Thus the unique feature of personhood appears to be captured by my characterisation.

Self-ascription is an identification of something with me (Everyone shall think of himself.). Either it is a definite description, which applies only to the relevant person or can easily be thus perfected. But, in the case of self-ascription, definite description differs in having a peculiar inadequacy. With any other definite description, one can expect to become acquainted with the thing described for the first time, for instance with a hotel room, in which I am supposed to spend the night, by specifying the city, the street, the number of the house, the floor and the room number. Only in the case of self-ascription does the right projection of the (ordered) pair, the relatum (what something is identified with), need to be familiar prior to the act of identification. Otherwise there would be an aimless infinite regress by constantly introducing new descriptions as explanantia, without ever revealing that it is I who is meant. For instance, in my case there would be a progression from a man born in Leipzig in 1928 to a professor emeritus of philosophy, in each case with the addition of information sufficient for definite description. In no case would it turn out that it is precisely I who is this individual; for all appropriate specifications of, on the one hand, Hermann Schmitz and, on the other, Alexander the Great contain nothing that would indicate that I am, e.g., Hermann Schmitz and not Alexander. In order to know this, I must already be acquainted with myself before any identification. Only in the opposite direction can this assertion become certain: if I am already acquainted with myself, I can, on the basis of experience and recollection of its circumstances, allot myself to my appropriate place in the world. If, in so doing, I am mistaken, for instance, in dreaming or because I am deluded, what I identify with myself is thoroughly out of order, but nothing changes about what I identify it with, namely myself; for I bring the acquaintance with myself to identification and hold onto it across all self-ascriptions.

So self-ascription is only possible if it is based on self-consciousness without identification. And such self-consciousness genuinely exists in the form of affective involvement. If I am, e.g., in pain, I immediately know it without having to find a sufferer to whom I ascribe identity with myself. Furthermore, there are states of upheaval or shock with increased or, on the contrary, reduced motion, in which the conscious subject has no access to itself as the referent of an identification but, nonetheless, distinctly feels itself in the intensity of excitement or derangement – e.g. raging anger, panicking fear, mass ecstasy, devoted struggle in the heat of the moment, being sunk in melancholy. The possibility of such a self-consciousness independent of such an identification is that facts of affective involvement are *subjective facts* which, apart from their mere factuality, have the mark of "Meinhaftigkeit" [mineness], to adopt a term coined by psychiatrist Kurt Schneider[1]. This can be seen in the fact that, at most, *one person*, namely the one affected, can assert such subjective facts, whereas everyone can do so for *objective* or (synonymously) *neutral facts*, as long as he is sufficiently knowledgeable and articulate. (The same is generally true for states of affairs, including non-factual ones.) This criterion is only read off the linguistic expression for purposes of terminological clarity but does not refer to anything particularly linguistic, since the range of linguistic expressions can be large but nonetheless insufficient to restate the subjective fact of an other's affective involvement. Let me take "I am sad" as an example. If someone else wants to express the same fact, he cannot use the first person singular but needs to say something like "Hermann Schmitz is sad". This I can restate, for instance, retrospectively, when I am no longer sad, replacing "is" by "was"; but if I want to describe the same fact as he does, I have to disregard the fact that I am Hermann Schmitz, for he could not say that, as he is not Hermann Schmitz. So now I have to deal with the fact that Hermann Schmitz is (or was) sad, disregarding the fact that I am Hermann Schmitz. But there is something missing about this fact that was expressed by my initial assertion "I am sad", namely the intensity of involvement with which sadness affects (or affected) me. And it is this nuance that is missing in the objective fact that the other could express

---

1   Schneider (1950, 130).

and which I can only express in my name. Yet, the content of both facts is the same, even the involvement is not missing in the objective fact, for if Hermann Schmitz is sad, he certainly is so in an involved manner. So the difference does not lie in the content but in the factuality. One has to part with the illusion that all facts are neutral or objective. Much rather, it is the case that there are not only many facts but also many factualities, namely one per conscious subject and one objective one that is shared by everyone and that comes into existence for someone by stripping it of subjectivity.

A critic tried to object by claiming that in both cases one has the same fact, once in one's own perspective and once in another's. This suggestion fails in that a fact which is subjective for someone is a subjective fact in another's perspective, too, and that an appropriate expression thereof is expected from him. This can be read from the use of the word "I". In representing objective fact not fraught with the speaker's affective involvement it functions as a mere pronoun that is superfluous, because it can be replaced by a name taking its place. If, for instance, I announce an objective fact to my friends by using the expression "Tomorrow Hermann Schmitz is coming, needless to say that it is I", one might wonder at the circuitous way of putting it, because ordinarily proper self-ascription is expected of every adult, but one will agree with me and accept my message as a complete representation of what I intended. If someone wants to stress the objectivity (or neutrality) of facts that he reports from his life, taking the position of a historian in his shoes, he will even avoid the first personal pronoun, as Caesar or Xenophon did when reporting on their campaigns. We have a different case if a subjective fact of one's own emotional involvement is to be communicated to someone else without loss. In that case, the word "I" no longer functions as a pronoun but as an indication of the subjectivity of what has been communicated by the speaker (no matter whether fact, desire or worry). I will show this by use of a few examples, for the purpose of which I will create the fictional character "Peter Smith". Take first a declaration of love: "Peter Smith loves you, needless to say that that is I." The girl spoken to is annoyed and possibly says: "Needless to say? That it is you is precisely what matters to me." A scene in a confessional: Sinner: "Peter Smith has sinned." Father: "Say, I have sinned." Sinner: "That isn't necessary." The father confessor refuses absolution. Finally a cry from the water: "Help, Peter Smith is drowning, needless to say that that is I." That is not a proper cry for help. The fellow man that would immediately have reacted to "Help, I'm drowning!" will first of all curiously investigate what the matter is.

The possibility of being self-conscious without an identification of something with oneself is based on the facts of affective involvement, even in their mere factuality, having the mark for the conscious subject of being-for-him as subjective facts, regardless of ascribable content. This is only possible if, in them, he, for whom they exist, is also found. He has to be given as identical to them without identification. The identity we have here is absolute identity, the opposite of difference, not yet the relative identity of something with something with which it is identified. The absolute identity of being this (and not that) cannot always be taken as given; in phases of dozing, many stages phase into one another. None is itself and different from others, but they all blend into one another. In absolute identity not requiring any identification, someone can find himself if what he encounters without leeway coincides with what happens to him. This happens in flinching, in strong embodied contraction, in the sudden dawning of something new, for instance, in fright, in an overwhelming twitch of pain, in a heavy jolt or gust of wind, if one is hit on the head or loses the ground under one's feet. Then the five elements *here, now, being, this* and *I* are rigidly joined in experience while orientation breaks down so that no features for the identification of something with something are available in this or that respect. This event I call the *primitive present*. On this, the subjectivity of the subjective facts of affective involvement is based, for in it he is found for whom these facts are subjective. But, as has been shown, the possibility of self-ascription, which would otherwise not have a relatum, is based on them. Thus, the person as a conscious subject with the capability of self-ascription is only possible by means of the primitive present.

Finding oneself prior to all identification is not restricted to the primitive present; one can also feel oneself in deep joy, but only because, in it, the primitive present is accessible as something that one masters by detaching from it. The same applies to any relaxed feeling of oneself. It is only possible as long as the resolution of contraction is experienced and, for instance, in cases of falling asleep or dozing off, it phases over into indifference and loss of self if that is no longer the case. For all other forms of affective involvement, the gap between finding oneself and the primitive present is bridged by the vital drive, which is the axis of embodied dynamism in the following sense:

When I say "felt-bodily" or "embodied", I am not speaking of the visible or tactile body but of the felt body as the carrier of such embodied impulses as, for instance, fear, pain, lust, hunger, thirst, disgust, vigor, tiredness and being in the grip of emotions. A further definitional clarification would be: *bodily/embodied* is whatever someone feels in the vicinity (not always within the boundaries) of their material body as belonging to themselves and without drawing on the senses, in particular, seeing and touching as well as the perceptual body schema (the habitual conception of one's own body), derived from the experiences made by means of the senses. The felt body has an idiosyncratic dynamic, the axis of which is the vital drive formed by the intertwined, tendencies of contraction and expansion; these, however, being partially separable. In this intertwinement, I characterise contraction as tension and expansion as swelling (in the sense of the strongly inflected participle "swelled", not its weak parallel form "swollen"); contraction that separates itself from the complex I shall call privative contraction and, accordingly, expansion that separates itself privative expansion. The fact that drive consists in the intertwinement of contraction and expansion running counter to one another can be shown as follows: it dissipates when the connection is broken; in fright, when contraction is suspended, it is frozen or paralysed. In falling asleep, in dozing or after ejaculation, when expansion phases out, it is lax. Sunken in on itself, the vital drive can be observed in pure form in the case of breathing. In the beginning, swelling is predominant but gradually and steadily gives way to tension; when it becomes unbearable, the drive is discharged into privative expansion by breathing out, that is, if it occurs without intermission. Through its openness to and its directability towards stimuli received, the pure drive is perfected to full vitality; then it is like steam that energises man like an engine.

The axis of embodied dynamism is the vital drive with its extensions by means of privative expansion and privative contraction towards expandedness or contractedness in the following sense: on this scale there is room for all embodied motions: the scale begins with privative expansion in fright. Due to an absence of antagonism between contraction and expansion, it is not really agonizing, but unsettling and annoying, since the drive is interrupted and needs to be re-threaded. Then there is a predominance of contracting tension in fear, pain, embarassing conflicts of a too forcefully repressed expansive impulse. We find it also in trepidation, hunger, disgust. This predominantly contracting vital drive is then followed by an approximate equilibrium of both competing tendencies in the exertion of strength (lifting, pulling, climbing) and breathing in. Further along the scale, swelling becomes predominant vis-à-vis the competing tension in lust (not only sexual, but also, for instance, in lust for scratching) and being in the grip of anger. After separation from tension, next along the scale, lies privative expansion, for instance, in the form of relaxation or beneficial tiredness. Apart from differences in weighting and the alternatives of intertwinement and separation, variations in the relation of contraction and expansion result from the form of binding in the intertwinement with the drive. It can be compact in the sense that tension and swelling do not come far apart, or in that the predominance shifts from one side to the other as, for instance, in the case of breathing in. The form of binding, however, can also be rhythmical fluctuation of the predominance of tension and swelling respectively, whereas the motion as a whole may nonetheless be marked by one or the other. In this sense, pain is compact; fear (with a predominance of tension) and lust (with a predominance of swelling), on the other hand, are rhythmical. This can be seen in the panting manner of breathing associated with fear and lust. In respiration, a swelling impulse breaks on the predominance of a repressing tension, and immediately resumes. Conversely, however, no one pants in pain.

What mediates between contraction and expansion is embodied directionality, for instance, as a gaze or breathing out, by irreversibly leading from contractedness to expansion, an expansion that neither, unlike swelling, is antagonistically intertwined with contraction nor, unlike privative expansion, sets itself off from it but can take the contraction with it, for instance, as a concentrated look or as a sudden pant. A further dimension of the felt body, apart from contraction and expansion, is that of protopathic (spreading in a dull and diffuse manner) and epicritical (becoming sharpened and more pinpointed) tendencies. The protopathic tendency is closer to expansion, whereas the epicritical tendency is closer to contraction. But there is also protopathic contraction (e.g. a sense of ponderation after excessive drinking) and epicritical expansion (e.g. a sprightly, springy step).

All affective involvement is primarily and originally embodied, an embodied stirring in the sense mentioned. One's personal way of dealing with it by giving in to or resisting it, can shape this affective involvement and give it a style, a personal touch. This affective involvement endows the personal as well as the pre-personal conscious subject with the possibility of consciously finding itself by means of the vital drive, which, together with elements of contraction, respectively expansion, makes the primitive present accessible by means of its contracting tendency. Without such access to the primitive present, which is a rare exceptional case, the gliding transition alternating from tension to swelling, together with privative expansion, does not reach the contour and clarity, which finds absolute identity in duration and space. By means of its overlapping with subjectivity in the primitive present, finding oneself without identification becomes possible. The dawning of the new has to tear apart the duration of perdurance and expose the present so that *this* as I, here, now and being provides identity; thus it is clear who can be affectively involved and identify themselves on this basis, no matter how determinately.

The vital drive does not only run through one's own felt body, but also gives rise to community in participatory embodied communication. It is already sketched in it from the beginning, in the form of the dialogue of the competing tendencies of tension and swelling. This dialogue is straddled into a drama with different characters. It already occurs in one's own felt body, when experiencing pain, which is not merely a state one is in, but also an imposing opponent with whom one has to grapple. Thus, it is different from fear, which is no less embarrassing. Fear and Pain are forms of an expansive drive, which is intercepted in an overwhelming manner. One can truly go with the experience of fear by, during panicked flight, going along with the impulse ("Away!") and nonetheless dragging along fear as an inhibition of the impulse. But one cannot truly go with the experience of pain; here discharging the impulse ("Away!") can only succeed symbolically in a cry breaking out and, inhibitedly, in motions of rearing up. Pain confronts and binds the person affected more radically than fear. The reason for this lies in its complicated tornness as a battle on two fronts that is expressed in the contrast between the partly expansive (crying, panting, rearing up) and the partly contracting (clenching fists, clenching one's jaw) pain gestures. The person affected wants to, on the one hand, expansively escape the pain and, on the other, by means of contraction, resists the expansiveness of pain itself, which presses and urges. Thus he is, so to speak, locked in by pain from two sides und thus forced to deal with it. The intracorporeal dialogue of contraction and expansion, in pain, begins to be straddled into a form of communication between partners. This straddling goes one step further in experiencing a sense of overpowering gravity when one trips, falls and only catches his balance at the last moment. This sense of gravity is a force with which he who falls resists, even though it does not confront him but is only felt by him in his own body, but not as its state, but as something foreign that haunts him. A similar case is an encounter with a strong headwind.

The straddling of embodied communication in the channel of the vital drive goes even further when it connects figures separated spatially, for instance, in exchanging glances: a glance in my direction contracts me, I return it, expansively bearing up against the contraction, and thus contract the other in such a manner that a shared vital drive of contraction and expansion connects us. A further example is the skillful evasion of a dangerously approaching bulky mass. This happens in a manner spontaneously adapted to the unforeseen circumstances, even though one hardly sees one's own body and cannot properly compare it to the imposing object with regard to position and distance. It succeeds because the glance as an embodied stirring of a type that irreversibly moves from contraction to expansion fixates on the imposing mass and integrates its suggested motion – the vivid sketch of the movement it is about to perform – into the body's motor schema[2] and to whose irreversible directions it itself belongs in such a manner that adaption in evasion becomes possible. Harmless and unnoticed, but much more complicated, this is the case when passers-by encounter one another on pavements. Everyone has only their own destination in mind, but careless glances are sufficient to avoid collisions, and everyone has to pay attention not only to the course of the immediate other but also to the others, coming into view behind and beside them.

Embodied communication of this kind, where a shared vital drive arises as a result of attending to a partner in communication, is what I call *antagonistic encorporation*. It is not only possible among felt bodies but also in relation to an inanimate object such as a stone thrown in one's direction or a dangerously approaching bulky mass. This is grounded in the bridging qualities that can be noticed in one's own felt body but also be perceived in encounters with others, whether at rest or in motion. These are suggestions of movement – vivid sketches of motion without being fully enacted – and synaesthetic qualities that are mostly intermodal properties of specific sensory qualities, but can, in the case of expansive, dense or pressing silence, also occur without any sensory quality. Synaesthetic qualities that do not require synaesthesia are, for example, the sharpness, luridness, softness, flashiness, brightness, hardness, warmth, coldness, gravity, massiveness, density, smoothness, roughness of colours, sounds, smells, of sound & silence, of a springy or sluggish gait, of joy, of enthusiasm, melancholy, freshness and tiredness; this list suggests how much overlaps in what is felt bodily and what is perceived objectively.

---

2   For a deeper insight into the motoric body plan, see Schmitz (2011, 21-23).

Antagonistic encorporation is partly one-sided when the dominant and binding contracting pole of the shared vital drive remains on one side, for instance, in the example given earlier of a dangerously approaching bulky mass or, with changing dominance, in exchanging glances and usually accompanying conversation. Mutual antagonistic encorporation is the source of spontaneous certainty which can occasionally also be misleading as regards dealing with another conscious subject.

Apart from antagonistic encorporation, there is also solidary encorporation, where a shared vital drive connects many individuals without anyone turning to any other. This is the case in frenzied courage or the panicked flight of a troop, in rhythmical calling, clapping, drumming by rhythm as its suggestion of motion that is tied to a succession as its successiveness, in joint singing, playing music, rowing or sawing, in mass ecstasy etc. Apart from encorporation as embodied communication in the channel of the vital drive, there is also embodied communication in the channel of privative expansion: this I call *excorporation*. Here we are dealing with trance-like states in which the contraction of the felt body, sustained by the contracting tendency, phases over into expansion. This can happen as an irreversible embodied directionality by staring into the depth of spaces, for instance, on monotonously straight roads, where a driver, whose vital drive is not very active, is in danger of losing control over his vehicle, or, so to speak, in a melting way, by dozing in the sun/staring into the light. This is a form of communication in which the felt body is absorbed; a reflux from the accessibility of the primitive present into cast expansiveness that is torn by an event of the primitive present.

From the gliding duration of persistence, not separated by duration and expandedness, with the primitive present that tears it apart, embodied dynamism, and embodied communication, a lifeform arises to which animals, infants, and people with advanced dementia are restricted. I say this with cautious regard for higher primates, e.g. apes; at best, an empirical zoologist, maybe not even he, can demarcate transitional stages where the notion becomes blurred. I call this life *life in the primitive present*. For this is the source from which not only the subjectivity of finding oneself without identification in affective involvement, but also identity radiates over the undeniably rich life in the primitive present. Moreover, we personal human beings live in the primitive present for the greater part, namely in all routine-based, spontaneous enactions which we share to a significant degree with animals. In so doing, in contrast to people suffering from apraxia after brain damage, we are protected from confusion in our motor routines. In this protection one can see that we are familiar with identity – here at first with absolute identity – and difference. But what is still missing is singularity. What is singular increases a number by 1. Identity without singularity can be illustrated using the example of chewing solid food smooth. Whoever chews, be it man or animal, in chewing he is familiar with the identity of the tongue and its difference from the food; for this reason, he does not chew his tongue. But in spontaneous chewing, something becomes singular only when something proves to be hard to chew and probably only for someone who is already a person. Coordinated movement would lose its flow if its elements became singular rather than phasing into one another.

Now we have reached a point where we can revisit the psychologistic-reductionist-introjectionist objectification, which was mentioned in the second hour and which was criticised for obscuring spontaneous life experience. We want to approach it from its foundation in psychologism. Psychologism is the idea that the entire experience of a conscious subject is enclosed in a private inner sphere, usually referred to as a soul. A decisive formulation and, at the same time, a pointer in the direction of the resulting problems is to be found in Kant: "If we let outer objects count as things in themselves, then it is absolutely impossible to comprehend how we are to acquire cognition of their reality outside us, since we base this merely on the representation, which is in us. For one cannot have sensation outside oneself, but only in oneself, and the whole of self-consciousness therefore provides nothing other than merely our own determinations."[3] The inner sphere has an owner, a conscious subject whose inner sphere it is. The next difficulty, which comes into view immediately as a consequence of the inner sphere's being closed off, consists in the conscious subject no longer being able to leave the sphere and check the testimony of his senses against the outside world. This was already noticed by Democritus, the first psychologist[4], and Kant, for this reason, even wants to locate all objects of whose reality someone can be certain in their inner sphere.

I do not want to focus on this problem here but rather want to attack psychologism with the charge that it cannot determine the relation of a conscious subject to their private inner sphere. To this end, four proposals

---

3   Kant (1998, 430 (A 378)).
4   Freeman (1948, 68B125).

have been made in the psychologistic tradition. The most rigorous of these is to equate the owner with the contents of the inner sphere, i.e. with a bundle of perceptions (Hume) or sensations (Mach); the early Husserl had similar ideas. This dissolution of the conscious subject is only tenable as long as one calmly sits in one's armchair; as soon as matters get serious, for instance, when one literally burns or is overcome by burning shame, one immediately notices that one is suffering and that it is not just a bundle of ideas that is undergoing modifications. Plato identifies the conscious subject with his soul, the entire inner sphere and, at the same time, locates the former within the latter, which leads to the paradoxical consequence that he portrays thinking as the soul soliloquizing with itself within the soul, as though an inhabitant of a house were the house in which he lives[5]. Aristotle identifies everyone, that is, the conscious subject, with the divine in him superseding humanity[6]; while this exaggeration, which is reminiscent of Nietzsche's "Übermensch", avoids Plato's contamination, it lacks credibility in its one-sided partiality. Finally, one can restrict the conscious subject to the ownership function, as does Kant, who sees the I as a subject without any recognizable determinations of its inner sphere, the I as object[7]. Likewise the (late) Husserl's pure I/Ego, "the pure Ego and nothing more", which is "an essentially different pure Ego for each stream of mental processes"[8]. Thus, one reduces the conscious subject to an empty form, just as Hume inflates it.

These suggestions are questionable in themselves. But all together they have a principal error: they come too late. They offer the conscious subject seemingly objective facts for self-ascription and condone the fact that it already needs to be acquainted with itself in order to be able to ascribe something to itself. In order – think of yourself! – for it to be I and not just anyone who is a bundle of ideas, a soul, a divine spirit or a pure I, I have to first of all be he whom I know prior to any self ascription, so that I enable it by proffering the relatum. Most traditional philosophers miss my point when they try to tell me who I am. If one wants to find what is sought after, one has to begin with what is known of the pre-knowledge that is brought to self-ascription. Then, as we have seen, one arrives at the subjective facts of an always already embodied affective involvement, then, in order to find him for whom they are subjective, to embodied dynamism in the form of the

---

5   Plato, *Laws*, 959a-b; *Sophist*, 263e3-5, 264a8 f.
6   Aristotle, *Nicomachean Ethics*, 1178a2-4 in combination with 1177b26-28.
7   Kant (1942, 270).
8   Husserl (1983, 191, 133).

primitive present and the vital drive. Thus, the foundation of personhood is not to be sought in the soul, but is embodied (of course, it isn't material either, like the brain is, which is now proffered as an ersatz for the soul by the neuroscientific heirs of the philosophical tradition). Embodied dynamism develops into embodied communication; from this results the bottom layer of personhood, life in the primitive present. In it, there is no being closed-off, there is much rather receptivity to the dawning of the new in the primitive present and a dialogue that is straddled into a play with various characters in the channel of the vital drive. In transcending the threshold to personhood, a private sphere evolves in the form of personal situation and personal world, opposing an alien sphere. This will be dealt with in the sixth hour. But this personal sphere is not sufficient to contain the conscious subject's entire experience as a private inner sphere, for that reason alone that this experience, including self-ascription, is only possible by the conscious subject's diving into the primitive present under the specifically personal.

Fourth Hour

Situations; The Unfolding of the Primitive Present into the World as
the Field of Possible Singularisation in Five Dimensions: Space, Time,
Being and Not-Being, Relative identity, What Is One's Own and What Is
Foreign; the Riddles of Time

Embodied dynamism and embodied communication are the most important sources of situations. A situation, in my sense of the term, is characterised by three features:

1. It is holistic, i.e. it is set off against the outside and hangs together internally.
2. It hangs together in virtue of a meaningfulness consisting of meaning. Meanings, in the sense intended here, are states of affairs (that something is the case), programmes (that something ought to / should be the case [as a norm or as a desire]) or problems (whether something is). (In using the term "is", for simplicity's sake, I here also refer to not-being, being-so and not-being-so. States of affairs can also be non-factual, as, for instance, in the case of illusory fear that something horrible is going to happen, when it does not.)
3. The meaningfulness is internally diffuse in the sense that within it not everything (possibly nothing) is singular, i.e. increases a number by 1.

Situations, in this sense, are, for instance, all motor competencies and their exertion, i.e. any goal-directed, spontaneous or planned movement of the body, for instance, in chewing solid food, in speaking or fighting off dangers. In such cases, a lot is understood (states of affairs), planned (programs) and resolved (problems) without more than a little of it consciously being perceived as particular (nothing in totally spontaneous exertions). For instance, someone who avoids a car crash on a road wet with rain in dense traffic by means of evasive manoeuvring, breaking or accelerating has grasped the relevant states of affairs and solved the problems of the impending crash. Likewise, he has instantaneously grasped states of affairs of possible additionally arising threats of a similar kind and programs for avoiding these (in antagonistic encorporation), and has answered them in a goal-directed manner without having had the time for the singularisation of the meanings involved, and if so, for a small fraction of them at best. In such cases, the entire meaningfulness of the situation is presented in one fell swoop; such situations I call *impressive*, otherwise (if only segments of meaningfulness transpire) *segmented*. I also call impressive situations polysignificant impressions. Another distinction concerning situations is that between *current* (which can be observed with a view to possible changes in time segments no matter how short) and *state-like* (in which searching for changes only makes sense after longer periods). All motor competencies are state-like situations, whereas their exertions are current ones.

The meaningfulness of current situations becomes particularly rich if someone has dealings with embodied creatures (animals or humans) in antagonistic or solidary encorporation. In the context of human communicative interaction – here we have current situations – languages are formed and change. Languages are state-like situations; in their entirety they consist in a holistic-internally diffuse meaningfulness composed of meanings that are programs, namely sentences. That is, they are rules about how one can speak in order to represent states of affairs, programs and/or problems. A competent user who has acquired the language draws on its stock of sentences and blindly but accurately selects those patterns that fit his communicative intentions; he is not picky before speaking but only in rule-following itself; only after speaking do they become accessible as particulars unless he is reciting a prepared text. Just as in the case of motor competencies, for instance, chewing solid food, as discussed in (III), in the case of speaking, we are dealing with a use (here of language) in the life in the primitive present protected by absolute identity and difference. In so doing, it is always only excerpts of the language commanded which become accessible. So it is a segmented situation, whereas the communicative exchanges in which language is used are often impressive situations. They can, however, also be segmented if the content of a conversation only surfaces in a fragmented manner (which meaningfulness is to be addressed respectively avoided in it).

Situations of encorporation among conscious subjects, for instance, in conversations full of nuances of dominance and submission are straddlings of the dialogic competition between tension and swelling in the shared vital drive by means of which their meaningfulness is significantly enriched. The exchanging of glances is of particular importance here, not, however, with a focus on intentions of dominance or submission, but rather on the automatism of the vital drive. The most dominant glances, as long as they are used naively and without manipulative intentions, are as far from the intention to dominate as possible: a loving and a humble glance are touching and disarming by knocking the ground from under the feet of the standpoint of the person affected. One cannot defend oneself without solid ground to stand on.

Life in the primitive present is full of situations, from the meaningfulness of which no individual meanings can be isolated. Instead, in this form of life, entire situations are conjured up, modified or answered by calls and cries. This form of life is not transcended before language in the form of sentences is acquired. I do not take this expression in a syntactic sense, as though such language needed to be grammatically structured, but in a semantic one: language has the form of sentences if it has the resources to isolate individual states of affairs, individual programs, individual problems from the meaningfulness of situations and/or to combine these explications. Communication in sentence form is a Janus-faced half-entity, a step that begins in the life in the primitive present and leads to what I will call life in the unfolded present. In relation to the language that uses it, as I have just shown, it takes root in the primitive present; in relation to the meanings that it situationally makes explicit and then recombines, however, in dealing with particulars, it draws on the unfolded present.

In the capacity for sentence-form communication lies the superiority of (personal) humans over animals. Humans can, at will, isolate and (re-) combine states of affairs, programs and problems that matter to them. Thus they can take charge of and reconstruct the situations from which they are drawn in such a manner as to be in control. By combining explicit meanings they can go beyond pre-given situations, re-arrange such constellations resulting from combination and, by means of such games, figure out what can be done in a situation and for what one should be prepared. Humans survive in their environment by reconstructing situations as constellations of individual factors without thus being able to exhaust the meaningfulness of situations; reconstruction remains a tentative adjustment by trial and error.

From the isolation of individual meanings in sentence-form communication the particularity of objects results in the following manner[1]: what is *singular* increases a number by 1 (or, logically equivalent: what is an element of a finite set). Numbers are properties of sets, sets the

---

1   Schmitz (2013, 23-47).

boundaries of classes in such a broad sense of the word that everything of which something can be an instance is a class[2]. Accordingly, something can only be singular as an element of a set and as an instance of a class. Classes are states of affairs that can only be identified as particulars; for only in this manner is it possible to determine which particular state of affairs is intended. This alone is sufficient to refute the claim of singularism (II) that everything, without prior conceptual prerequisites, is singular (exceptions being 'being an element' or 'being the case'). At best, the partial claim that everything is singular could be true, but it, too, can be refuted, not only empirically, for instance, by pointing to a period of dozing (III), but also at a purely logical level[3]. Every class is a determination by means of which something is specified as a case of something; every determination is a class in this broad sense. The determination has to apply to what is determined in such a manner that what is determined is endowed with the determination; both applying to and being endowed with, is the same relation, seen from the other side. However, applying to, in turn, is a determination of the applying determination. From this it follows that the relation is complicated by intermediary links. They unfold into a chain without end, an infinite progression; for applying to, in turn, has the determination of applying to the applying determination; so a second applying to is added to the first, a third to the second and so on. Thus the possibility of being endowed with a determination is foreclosed; for what is being endowed with the determination would have to be the first link in the chain that ascends to the applying determination, i.e. the last link in the chain when descending. But a chain running into infinity does not have a last link. Accordingly, everything would be undetermined. Of course, this is false, just like the whole line of reasoning. The mistake lies in the presumption that every determination is singular, i.e. that, as a link in a chain, it increases the number of the links by 1. From this it follows that there can be no object the determinations of which (be it of applying to or being endowed with) are singular in their entirety. All singular determinations are embedded in a mist of non-singular ones. The singularist presumption that everything is singular cannot be maintained for the determination of any singular object.

---

2   On the notions of case and class, see ibid (43 et seq.).
3   Ibid. (69-76).

So something can only be singular if its absolute identity of being itself is complemented by the characterisation as an instance of a (singular) class[4], and a singular class or determination is only possible against the backdrop of a diffuse plethora of determinations that are or contain meanings (states of affairs, programs, problems); i.e. this background cannot consist solely of singular entities. This plethora could be shapeless, as it appears in states of severe drowsiness; for animals and humans it only becomes manageable in dealing with it as an internally diffuse holistic meaningfulness of situations. But the holistic character of situations does not always come along with singularity. Every human constantly goes through situations to which he smoothly adapts, but they only become singular in retrospect, for instance, if one considers whether one has already experienced something of the like or something similar. Many humans, for instance, children in pre-school, speak a language without noticing that it is a singular language. A holistic structure without singularity is more clearly to be found in the case of smoothly flowing complex motor routines. So the holistic character of situations is prior to singularity or numerical unity, even if many situations are singular or, at least, can be singularised.

Singular meanings are only possible through their isolation out of the internally diffuse meaningfulness of situations by means of sentence-form communication. States of affairs (see page 76, footnote 2), which commonly contain programs and/or problems, are classes or determinations of something that is their case. They have to be singular in order to determine a set as the extension of a certain, singular class in such a manner that the instance/case can be singular as an element of a set. From this it follows that sentence-form communication is a condition of the possibility of singular entities. Singularity is the complementation of absolute identity by the determination as a case/instance of a singular class (determination) that has a set as its extension, i.e. an extension that has a number. This role can be played by many, often unfathomably or infinitely many classes. Thus the absolute identity of being this and nothing else is expanded into the relative identity of something with something. What is singular as an instance of A is identical with it as an instance of B etc. The trivial borderline case of relative identity is identity with itself under the same aspect, i.e. tautology.

---

4   The corollary that, in order to be singular, every class requires another class, a case of which it is, et cetera ad infinitum, is not correct. On this issue, see Schmitz 2008a, 42.

After singularity has been made out as the mode in which absolute identity is elaborated into relative identity, we can now assume a perspective of a framework, in which there is room for everything that is salient about situations and can be gleaned from them. This framework is the *world* as the field of free singularity, i.e. the possible singularisation of something. Here it is not essential that it is, in fact, possible to singularise everything, to fathom the background of the situation marked by internally diffuse meaningfulness through the constellation of singular factors. That would be the error of singularism (II) and constellationism, which may be popular in modern technocratic thinking, but which, as we have seen, digs its own grave. Man is fated to approximately reconstruct situations as constellations; this is his birthright, for otherwise he could not assert himself. But in doing so, he is well advised to keep in mind and respect the internally diffuse meaningfulness of the situations on which he draws. Cultivating this respect into a special form of explication in sentence-form communication is the task and an achievement of poetry. While the prosaic explication, following the prototype of problem solving, isolates only a fact or a valid program as the solution and forgets everything else, the poet, from the states of affairs, programs and problems, in elegant austerity weaves a net so thin that the situational network invoked by him, especially in extended and complex lyrics, transpires in its entirety. Poetry, considered a flighty rendering of a rough reality, is often not taken seriously and even less so under the auspices of a viral constellationism; but the poets way of seeing and working, of letting the holistic structure of situations and their internally diffuse meaningfulness shine through and take effect by means of the explicantia gained in communication is, at the same time, the foundation for the able practitioner and agent of human commerce, be he a politician, a tradesman, a manager, a doctor, an officer, a nurse, an educator or any other profession involving dealing with (groups of) humans. If, however, he sacrifices this hermeneutic intelligence, which requires only very little explication in crucial points, in favour of a more analytical one, which contents itself with explications and their combination, he will fail.

By entering the world, the horizon of a life in the primitive present is transcended. This does not mean entering a new territory with a fundamentally different order though, for the framework that the world sets up for the possibilities of singular existence can be construed as the unfolding of the five elements which are indistinguishably fused in the primitive present: here, now, being, this, I. So entering the world, which for subjectivity, being and identity remains tied to the primitive present, is also an unfolding of this (primitive) present. Life in the world is a *life in the unfolded present*. I want to retrace this unfolding in the order of the five elements.

1. The *here* of the primitive present, absolute location, as embodied contraction of threat in view of a sudden dawning of the new, unfolds into a system of relative locations, which, by means of specification of position and distance, mutually determine one another in the manner of a coordinate system. This system can, at will, be opened up over the expanse, from which contraction is expelled by means of contraction, as a frame, in which everything that is suitable for singularisation is determined as a locationally definite singularity.

2. The *now* of the primitive present, the absolute moment of the sudden dawning of the new, correspondingly unfolds by means of a series of relative moments, which are partly positioned in the new by expectation and partly, by memory, in the interrupted duration of "Dahinleben" [subsisting], which is terminated by the interrupting departure and no longer exists. Thus a relational temporality emerges as an array of events by the relation of earlier to later or what happens at the same time (i.e. occurs in the same moment); in this array the absolute moment is levelled off to a mere stage in the series, a relative moment amongst others. This array of events (or of particular things of another kind) by the relation of earlier to later or simultaneity I call *pure relational temporality*; it serves singularisation by fixing dates, just as localisation does in spatial regards. But relational temporality does not remain pure; it is contaminated by the admixture of the categorisation of events (and other things) into future (which have not happened yet), present (which are neither no longer not yet nor not yet no more) and past (which are no more). This categorisation is the trail of the happening of the primitive present in time. This occurrence, the sudden dawning of the new, in transition, holds together present and future: present in which that, what is new, occurs, interrupting duration, and future in which that, what is new, is new by letting that, what is yet to be, occur in the process of happening. In the happening in the primitive present, by contrast, the past is not mixed with the present, for it is the fate of duration interrupted by the dawning of the new, which in passing fades into no longer being and is separated from the present by this departure. This structure, on the one hand mixed, on the other separated, is smoothed out into the three homogenous sets of past, present and future

in the unfolding of the primitive present into the world. Thus arises, next to relative temporality, a *modal temporality*, i.e. a temporality that is characterised by modal differences of being, not-yet-being and no-longer-being. This *modal temporality*, together with *pure relational temporality*, is blended into a modal relational temporality by accommodating the present in one of the relative moments of pure relational temporality, from which the future is later and the past earlier. On this modal relational temporality is imprinted the *flow of time* which consists in the fact that the past (considered as the amount of things that have happened in the past) constantly grows, the future (the amount of things that will happen in the future) constantly shrinks (even if it were infinite) and the present (in the sense of the amount of what is presently the case) is constantly shifting. The modal features of not-yet-being and no-longer-being would in themselves admit of interruptions in the transition into being or not-being; the fact that this transition is uninterrupted makes it a flow.

The blending of relational temporality with modal temporality to a modal relational temporality, with a corresponding flow of time, brings such difficulties and aporias with it that I will only come back to the issue with an extensive comment after having mustered the five modes of unfolding.

3. The *being* of the primitive present unfolds into an element of a distinction applicable to everything without difference, by being juxtaposed to not-being in its entire breadth. By contrast, as an element of the primitive present, it is only juxtaposed to the no-longer-being of interrupted duration. The shape of singularity transcends the threshold from being to not-being; thus it becomes possible to also find singularity in not-being. For this reason, people can playfully identify themselves with something if they live, plan, expect, remember, hope, fear, imagine in the unfolded present. The above mentioned characteristic feature of humans to transcend situations in a planned manner by exploratively rearranging sets of networks that reconstruct these situations is based on the transition of singularity into non-being. Thus the world, as the field of free singularity, does not end at the border of not-being.

Even though being has a different format in the unfolded present than it does in the primitive present, one can hardly say that it has completely emancipated itself from the latter. Humans would be clueless if they had to deal with the difference between being and not being without drawing on the accessibility of the primitive present. This results from the fact that being, unlike colour or sound, can neither be read off objects as something belonging to them nor can it be introduced by use of a conceptual feature, the specification of necessary and sufficient conditions. This results from the two sentences (A) and (B), for which I will now provide a proof.

(A) Being is not an attribute of anything, i.e. it is nothing that is essential to the identity of an object by contributing to determining that it is this object, and not another.

(B) There is no criterion of being, i.e. there is no non-circularly specifiable necessary, and sufficient condition for the fact that something is.

Proof of (A): Every object necessarily has its attributes, for it is necessarily identical with itself, it is this and no other. No object can be specified by attributes other than those that, in fact, are its attributes. Even though there might be exceptions in the domain of subjective facts[5], it is sufficient to prove (A) for objective facts. If existence were an attribute of an object, it would have to exist. But it can easily be shown that nothing exists of necessity. For in that case it would be impossible for nothing to exist. This could only be impossible if it entailed a contradiction. This would have to be revealed by the impossibility of non-contradictorily mentally representing everything as not-being. A contradiction could only occur if something were doubly represented as being and not-being. But this is not the case if everything is represented as not-being and only as not-being. So this representation is non-contradictory. But then it is possible that nothing exists. Then being cannot be an attribute. From this it also follows that nothing that would lead one to posit existence (an existence-inductive) can be an attribute. Existence-inductives are specifications, for which, if they were attributes of an object, it would be necessary that an object (this or another) exists (including past and future existence). Existence-inductives, apart from being itself, are past, present, future, the truth of existential propositions, the factuality of states of affairs concerning existence, authorship. From (A) it follows that one cannot find being in a singular object, for in it one can find only what belongs to it, i.e. what is relevant for its identity as this object.

Proof of (B): (B) follows from (A). A criterion of being would be a feature by means of which a being object is distinct from a not-being object. But as being is not an attribute, every being object has at least one not-being counterpart that has exactly the same attributes, that is, in everything that belongs to its being this and not another object. Then

---

5   Schmitz (2013, 37).

there can be no feature of the kind sought after[6]. In addressing the aporias of time, I will give an illustrative example of such a counterpart: a past object compared with it as present.

From (A) and (B) it follows that people are only familiar with being in contrast to not-being in virtue of the contracting tendency of the vital drive, which makes the primitive present accessible. Otherwise, they would miss the distinction, as it happens when one is dreaming or one is immersed in pure mathematics, where it is sufficient for the existence of an object that it follows from arbitrary but non-contradictory assumptions, i.e. is possible[7]. But not even from the primitive present as a singular object can being be read off, for it is not a singular object, but is only turned into one retrospectively from a position of the unfolded present, with a balancing and correcting influence from the knowledge of what is inappropriate in this view.

4. The _this_ of the primitive present, the absolutely identical unfolds by means of the complementation of absolute identity onto relative identity of something with something, i.e. in virtue of the fact that, in each case, many classes, characterisations and aspects are available, under which something can be seen as an instance of something in such a manner that, as a case of this, it is identical with itself as a case of that. Thus life in the unfolded present gains a flexibility that plays into the hands of man's strategic competence of rearranging reconstructively cast nets of constellations.

5. The _I_ of the primitive present, the conscious subject entangled in the facts of affective involvement, which are subjective for him, who is shaken and challenged by the sudden dawning of the new, unfolds through complementation of its absolute identity to singularity as a matter of characterisation and becomes a singular subject, around whom a personal sphere emerges in contrast to what is alien. Alienation comes into existence via the neutralisation of meanings, the peeling off of subjectivity from states of affairs, programs and problems. I will address these issues in more detail in the sixth hour.

---

6   Since 1964, I long-held thesis (B) using an argumentation which actually suffered from an inadequacy that came to my attention just recently when it took me a lot of effort to convince a benevolent listener. Two days later, just having woken up, the proof imparted here came to my mind; 15 minutes later I had it figured out.

7   In a letter written to Gottlob Frege on December 29th, 1899, David Hilbert wrote: "If the arbitrarily set axioms do not contradict each other, with all consequences, then they are true, then the things formulated by the axioms exist." (Gabriel et al. 1976, 66; translation by Martin Bastert).

Now I want to return to the second point, the unfolding of the *now* of the primitive present and the particular difficulties associated with it. Of the four other modes of unfolding, one can say that the process has been achieved in a smooth and uninterrupted manner. The primitive present can recede into inconspicuity until it resurfaces in sudden involvement. In locational space one can orient oneself, where something is, where it is moving etc., without considering the absolute location of the primitive present. One can deal with being in passing, pit not-being against being and vice versa in a planned manner, without considering the source of acquaintance with being or remembering it. It is common to take singularity and its concomitant relative identity for granted, without seeing that it would break down if the primitive present didn't plant absolute identity in duration and expanse. On the subjective side of unfolding, the personal subject behaves in such an assured manner that it forgets as well as denies that for self-ascription it remains tied to the primitive present; before me no one has dealt with embodied dynamism. In these four directions, the unfolding of the primitive present works so well that one could fail to see it. Only the unfolding of temporality failed and, so to speak, got stuck half-way. Locational space would correspond to relational temporality, but the latter is hindered from smoothly covering up (even hiding) the primitive present by being burdened by modal temporality in conjunction with the flow of time. Thus result the tragic characteristics of the flow of time, which imbue life with brokenness and lability: the uncertainty of what is to come, the fleeting changes of the present, the violence of parting with what no longer is. Even more intellectually disturbing are the contradictions that give the flow of time a scent of impossibility.

Contradictions have long since been attributed to time, even though well-founded arguments have been lacking. By use of dramatic rhetoric, Augustine embellishes the sceptics' argument that there can be no time, since in time only the present is real, but merely is a point without duration. The sceptics assume that a single present moment stands between not-being future and not-being past. As soon, however, as one considers that the present is constantly changing and, in each case, a different amount of the present fills the moment, this changing itself turns out to be what has duration. Against this, the argument turns out to lose its point. It denies the dynamism of the flow of time in favour of a static abstraction. An objection by McTaggart became famous in the 20th century, according to which the reality of time could be called into question because of the seeming contradiction that every event in time is simultaneously in the past, present and future, even though these predicates are mutually exclusive. In making this objection, he confuses "and" with "or"[8]. But there are also objections which call the flow of time into question more seriously.

Certainly, Caesar was murdered. But in history everything is uncertain; it could, for instance, be the case that, before being stabbed by a dagger, he succumbed to a heart attack; the sources could also be misleading. So there is a point to hypothetically distinguishing Caesar's true murder from a falsely assumed murder, even though there is no reason to doubt the fact that he was murdered. Both events, the real one and the falsely assumed one, overlap in all their attributes. Caesar's true murder is past. His true murder is also identical with his past murder. However, his true murder is real but his past murder is not, as it is no longer real. Leibniz's law (the identity of indiscernibles), according to which identical objects are determined by the same characterisations, breaks down in the case of this example. It holds only for attributes, not for existence-inductives, and the past is an existence-inductive. (I use the terms "being", "reality" and "existence" synonymously.) This paradox can be presented in various versions. We remember what has been the case. The presence of the latter is part of this. Especially for all practical actions, for instance, murdering Caesar, it is necessary that they have an effect on the present, while observing something theoretically can be equally well directed towards the past, the future or the atemporality (e.g. mathematical entities). But an event that is past is no longer present and no longer exists at all. The same goes for a past age. So we can remember nothing of the kind, for if we take it in its present we deny the past, and if we assume the past we put ourselves in opposition to the present as a necessary part of what we remember. (I hardly need to say that one does not do anything to resolve the difficulty by temporally relativating reality, for instance, by saying that Caesar's murder was real in 44 B.C. but not real in 2008 A.D., for reality at a time has nothing to do with reality but with fixing a date in relational temporality, as can be seen from the fact that the respective time, too, for instance, the age of Caesar and with it the reality at this time is no longer real.) Yet another version has it that nothing changes by passing away, as exactly the same thing that passed away was present, even though it discards its present character and takes on the character of the past. Finally, one can express the contradiction by saying that past present is impossible, since past and present, no-longer-being and being are exclusive; on the other hand, however, the past is not possible without a past present. What I have said here about the past and memory holds equally for the future and expectation.

---

8   For a more detailed examination see Schmitz (2014, 173-176).

A further paradox directly concerns the flow of time, the fact that the amount of everything that is in the past grows continuously, the amount of everything in the future shrinks and the amount of everything in the present is changing constantly. This happens in virtue of the fact that the constantly changing present eats its way into the future at the tip of what has passed. This is a process. Each process has a stage that it reaches in each case, as long as it is happening. What is the stage of the flow of time? When does the present arrive? An answer is possible in two ways. One can say that the present reaches, for instance, the 1st of Jan 2000 on the 1st of Jan 2000, and similarly so for all dates, but these are uninformative tautologies, which only express the idea that, in each case, the present occurs at that moment of relational temporality at which it occurs. A different way of arriving is more informative: the changing present arrives now, in the present. But then the former cannot be identical with the latter, for that would not be a process of reaching itself. On the other hand, the changing present cannot be different from the one at which it arrives, for then it would not be now, not present.

A way out of these conundrums that would seem to be suggested might be to call into doubt the being of modal relational temporality, to discard it as an illusion. This path has often been chosen – in our age particularly by physicists in the wake of the general theory of relativity – but the sacrifice would be too great. Without modal relational temporality there would be no learning, for learning consists in experiencing something that one did not yet know in such a manner that one's state of knowledge is no longer identical to the one one had formerly, which is now past. But without a willingness to learn, no scientist is possible, for he has to, at least, be prepared to learn from being challenged by himself and others, whether his claims stand up to criticism; otherwise he is no scientist but a dogmatist who lays claim to absolute correctness of what he believes to be correct. Especially natural science is dependent on modal relational temporality, for it confirms its theories by means of experiments, and experiments are only possible in virtue of the fact that, when beginning an experiment, one does not yet know whether the theoretical prediction will be confirmed. But not only scientific thought, also human thought on the whole requires modal relational temporality. The kind of temporality that would be left after subtracting modal features and the flow of time would be a pure relational temporality. In it, rather than directed relations of something to something, there are only complex relations which can be read off equally well from two sides, from the earlier to the later and from the later to the earlier. If simultaneity is furthermore taken into account, the two-sidedness becomes an unforeseeably complex many-sidedness. Grasping complex relations without splitting them into relations would be a feat of an intuitive mind, as Kant ascribed it to God; man can only think discursively by carrying directed relations of something to something into them. This is said more easily than it is done. A direction can only be found by setting out from one's point of origin to one's goal, be it bodily or mentally; in order to find the way, however, a direction already needs to be given. Otherwise, one is confronted cluelessly with a choice, for which the complex relation affords no opportunity. This cluelessness can only be resolved if a direction is given by guidance without one's own involvement. In the light of complex relations, human thought has nothing to draw on but the flow of time, if only in the shape of the brief time that passes, while the thinker moves from one segment of the relation to the next. Moreover, every directed process would fulfil the same function, but processes are only possible in the flow of time. Without it, only complex relations remain, at best monotonous functions of the kind encountered in mathematical exponentiation, where higher values of the independent variable consistently correspond to even greater values of the dependent one.

One will have to live with modal relational temporality. But this cannot happen by allowing a contradiction to persist; for a contradictory sentence – a sentence that has a contradiction as its logical consequence[9] – takes back everything it claims and, in effect, asserts nothing. The saving way out of the undeniable contradiction in describing an unquestionably given fact consists in fobbing the contradiction off from the description to an ambiguity in the state of affairs, and finding a non-contradictory description for the latter. In order to illustrate what I take 'ambiguity' to mean, I like to draw on an event that Edmund Husserl experienced as a student and which obviously did not let go of him, since he kept returning to it at different stages of his life. In a waxworks cabinet he, at least for the fragment of a second, saw a hybrid of a lady and a wax figure. Two incompatible appearances were competing with one another for the identity of a third. After a short while, the ambiguity was resolved; Husserl noticed that it was a wax figure. Such confusing overlappings – I speak of the Husserlian figure here – have also been reported by other contemporaries. In our experience we are then dealing with fleeting illusions; but one can imagine a possible world, which is riven with many mysteries of such a kind, and which, in principle, cannot be resolved because mystery lies at the heart of the

---

9   Concerning the term "logical consequence" see Schmitz (2008a, 98).

matter, an ambiguity that could be expanded into a polyvalence for n > 2. The attribute, all or some, would, in principle, be undecidable alternatives (to stay with the simplest case n=2) which, as in Husserl's experience, obfuscate one another by competing for identity. This conflict cannot be resolved by an "either … or", for then the decision would be right for one alternative, as in Husserl's case when he realised the illusion. Much rather, the mode of being of such a thing is marked by an undecided hovering state, in which incompatible characterisations run counter to one another, not a state of mere indeterminacy though, but rather a state overloaded by determinations, none of which becomes predominant.

I have introduced this thought experiment to point a way out of having to grant a contradiction in correctly describing a state of affairs. The contradiction is fobbed off to the thing described as a confusion, which is its nature. Such confusion is non-contradictory. For if a true contradiction, a sentence of the form "A and not A" (for any sentence A) is at hand, it follows from the law of the excluded middle that one of the conjuncts is correct; in describing an ambiguity of the kind mentioned, this does not follow, since both conjuncts are competing for identity, although neither is triumphant with regard to factuality or truth. Now the question is how to describe such an ambiguous but non-contradictory state of affairs. Simple undecidedness cannot be the solution, for this could be mere indeterminacy, as in dozing, when no phase of gliding crystallises as singular, because the requisite determinate structure is missing. Now one can iterate the undecidedness into an undecidedness whether it is undecided, whether things are thus or so (e.g. whether a lady or a wax figure is there). Thus one has excluded simple undecidedness, for if this were the case at hand, one would not have to ascend to the twofold undecidedness; what is definitively excluded is unambiguous decidedness that we are dealing either with a wax figure or a lady; in that case, nothing would be factually undecided. But so much exclusion is not sufficient, for by means of it the field of open indeterminacy would be expanded, while it is, at the same time narrowed down by competing criss-crossing. Continuing to higher levels of finite-fold undecidedness is no help here. It is not adequate to the competition for identity, the overlapping without possibility of setting itself off prevented by the criss-crossing. A satisfactory description is only reached when one goes on to infinite-fold undecidedness. As one cannot subtract from infinity, infinite-fold undecidedness leaves everything open concerning unambiguous decidedness, simple undecidedness, undecidedness whether something is undecided, furthermore whether it is undecided whether it is undecided whether it is undecided etc. to infinity. Here undecidedness is meant as the constitution of the object, not the judgement. If everything remains open, nothing is decided, neither about decidedness (i.e. the absence of ambiguity) nor about an undecidedness referring to it through a sequence of ascending steps, and an unrestricted playing field remains open for the incompatible aspects of the ambiguity, which cannot be restricted, but not because its relation is too loose, but because it is too close in competition in order to still speak of undecidedness (of a finite stage) in contrast to decidedness. Infinite-fold undecidedness is infinitely weak undecidedness, because, with every step to a higher stage of undecidedness, it becomes more undecided, i.e. measured according to decidedness, it becomes weaker. In the grey area of competition, every scale for setting the degree of undecidedness fails; and in order to describe this complicated state of affairs, the only solution is a transition to an infinite-fold undecidedness.

In my logic of iterated undecidedness[10] I have developed a procedure that allows one to reinterpret contradictions as ambiguities of states of affairs that are, in themselves, confused and which can, as such, be described in a non-contradictory manner. Applied to the contradictions read off from the flow of time, the procedure yields the insight that it is weakly undecided whether Caesar's true murder is or is not, whether we can remember it whether present can be past, whether the changing present is identical to the present that is now. This last question is reminiscent of one of Schopenhauer's reflexions, which insightfully elucidates the ambiguity between the changing present that arrives now and the present at which it now arrives: "At times I feel astonished about the present and the question arises: why is this now precisely now?"[11] Through a mishap in the unfolding of the primitive present on the temporal side of the absolute moment (as opposed to relational temporality) the unfolding of modal relational temporality got caught in ambiguous criss-crossing which makes a non-contradictory description impossible, as long as one does not grant the ambiguity as the true nature of the matter. The difficulties with logical antinomies (e.g. the set theory, the liar paradox) that I have defused with simple undecidedness in easy cases and with infinite-fold undecidedness in more difficult cases, so that the naïve set theory developed by Cantor can be revisited in its whole extent, without restriction through the defensive axiomatic systems to fend off contradictions[12].

---

10   Schmitz (2013, 123-132).
11   Schopenhauer (1863, 731).
12   Schmitz (2013, 133-137).

V
Fifth Hour
Stages of Spatiality: Spaces Containing Surfaces and Surfaceless Spaces; the Spatiality of the Felt Body and Emotions; Emotions as Half-Things; Feeling Emotions; Law, Morality and Religion; the Surface as the Alienation of Space from the Felt Body

At the same time as the psychologistic-reductionist-introjectionist objectification (II), Greek geometry develops, which conceives of and thematises space primarily as surface, within which it constructs by means of rulers and compasses. Thus it lays the foundation for the conception of space that is predominant to this day. It is a conception of three-dimensional space in which there are, apart from surfaces, points and lines and three-dimensional bodies. All these figures are found in surfaces and are only accessible from there: lines as edges in touching surfaces or being drawn into surfaces, points in refraction or convergence of lines, three-dimensional bodies by placing fringed surfaces adjacent to one another and dividing the circumferential space by intersectional surfaces. But this holds only for bodies as three-dimensional constructs; actual embodiment, i.e. voluminosity is experienced differently (independently of the dimension), as will shortly be seen. Three-dimensionality can only be characterised by means of points and lines in bodies felt and seen[1], usually with an intersection of three straight lines in a point. While points, surfaces and three-dimensional objects only become accessible through the surface, surfaces are immediately present. Of course, they are mostly found as surfaces of bodies, but this happens accidentally. Sun and Moon are optically given as surfaces (even if they are not) like the rainbow; it will be no problem for modern technology to represent even light surfaces as surfaces without background in bodies. Thus, our usual concept of space has surface as its basis.

In surfaces there are points which can be connected by reversible lines. One can read locations and (reversible) distances off these lines and

---

1   The same can also be said about the applicability of Menger's abstract topological term dimension to illustrative bodies. For more information about this matter see Schmitz (1967, 373-391).

construct a system of locations over them, which mutually determine one another through the distances and locations of the objects located there, i.e. they make one another identifiable. Space is construed as a network of such locations, the density of which, like a coordinate system, can be increased as one sees fit. As it turns out, it is exactly three-dimensional, i.e. no constructs with higher dimensionality than points, lines, surfaces and bodies are contained in it. Movement is characterised as change in location, rest as remaining in the same location. Natural science and common sense adopt this conception of space.

But logically it is faulty, because it is based on a definitional circularity. The places which are determined by positions and distances have to be determined by locations and distances to motionless objects. For if they moved, their locations and the distances to them would change. The location would have become another and the objects positioned at it would have changed their place, even if they had remained at rest. As rest is characterised as remaining in one place, they would have been at rest and not at rest. They would have changed their location. So according to the definition, they would have moved without moving. In order to avoid such contradictions, motionless objects of reference need to be chosen for the calibration of locations by means of positions and distances to them. Thus, location presupposes motionlessness (rest), but motionlessness (rest) presupposes location if it is construed as remaining in the same place. This is a definitional circularity that de-values the conception of space as it was previously sketched here. But one can develop a clearer conception of it by means of the presupposed foundational concept of place – a task that, to date, has strangely been neglected. A place of the given kind is a relative location, determined by relation to objects of reference. Here I speak of *relative places*. A system of relative places which mutually determine one another by positions and distances is what I call a *locational space*. Let F be the period throughout which a locational space persists. If we, like Newton or Euler, are dealing with an absolute universal space, F is the duration of the universe; if locational space is relative to a coordinate system, as for instance, in those according to Galileo or Einstein, we are dealing with a duration that is stipulated for the coordinate system. An object is in one location throughout a period (of time). This would be a three-place relation. As it is easier to treat being in a location as a two-place relation, I will express myself in such a manner that the ordered pair (g; f), consisting of an object as first entry and a period (of time) as second entry, is in the location. I say that the ordered pair has a position and a distance to an object if its first entry has it. The relative location of the pair (g; f), where f is a partial duration of F (possibly F), can be determined as the set of all those ordered pairs with an object as first entry and a partial duration of F (possibly F) as second entry which have the same location and distance relations throughout the whole period F as (g; f), i.e. as g throughout f. As this is an equivalence relation in the mathematical sense, it ensures that no object can be positioned at more than one location at any one time[2]. Of two relative places I say that they have a position and a distance to one another if this holds true for first entries of ordered pairs positioned there. Then it holds true for all relative places of the respective locational space that they mutually determine one another by means of the positions and distances of the objects positioned there.

So the common conception of space is faulty from a logical point of view. But what went wrong? Obviously rest has to be presupposed as given in introducing a spatial structure on the basis of surface and cannot be introduced at a later stage as remaining in one relative place. Here it can be seen how misleading it was to exclusively orient the conception of space towards spaces containing surfaces. For, amongst spaces, there are also surfaceless spaces and in them a kind of rest that is not dependent on locations. A surfaceless space is, for instance, the space of sound in which sonorous and droning sounds expand widely, where shrill whistling sounds contract in a sharp manner, where suggestions of motion such as rhythm and other gestures of sound, for instance, a fanfare, sketch movements which more or less take hold of the hearing felt body. High and low pitches of sound occur just like a distance without a reversible distance, as one spontaneously notices whether a sound is farther away than another, but not, as in seeing, how far away one is from it. The space of festive or oppressive silence; the one is farther away, the other is heavier, but both are denser than the equally as expanded soft and expansive silence of the morning. The space of wind that hits one is also surfaceless, it has a motion that is free of locational change, that is, as long as one does not reinterpret the experienced wind, a half-entity as air, a full entity. Also surfaceless is the unnoticed back field of which one constantly makes use in forward-directed activity by leaning back, stretching and bending. Surfaceless is the space of the weather that one experiences, for instance, when one leaves a stuffy chamber and breathes freely in the open and enters an atmosphere in which the perceiving felt body can unfold better than previously. It achieves it with

---

2   Schmitz (2013, 149 et seq.).

a freely unfolding gesture and the space of the latter is also surfaceless. The space of embodied stirrings is also surfaceless, for instance, of an addled brain, of breathing in and out, of freshness and tiredness. A final surfaceless space is that of water, as it is experienced by swimmers or divers, as long as they are not visually oriented and do not project mental images of their own or other delimited material bodies into what is encountered. In the water there are no surfaces, points, lines and thus no three-dimensional bodies. There is, however, volume which more or less presents a resistance against which they have to struggle if it does not gently support them. Water has a volume that is not three-dimensional but is dynamically composed of tension and swelling, which are marked by privative expansion if it presents itself as a gently supporting element. It is a volume of the same kind as is felt when breathing in, with a chance of phasing over into privative expansion comparable to breathing out. The isomorphism is based on the shared vital drive of antagonistic encorporation. This dynamical, not-three-dimensional volume, is the spontaneously experienced embodiment that endows what is solid as well as what is liquid, but also sound and the felt body (e.g. in the felt gravity of tired limbs) with a massiveness that has to be added to three-dimensional constructs for them to make an impression as complete bodies.

Due to a lack of surfaces, in surfaceless spaces there are no points, lines and three-dimensional constructs. Also, there are no reversible connecting lines off of which one could read positions and distances. However, there is a dynamical volume with suggestions of motion and directions that are not reversible but refer to the absolute location of the felt body by starting from or meeting it, for instance, in the directions of glances. What I term *absolute location* is the location of a felt body as long as it is not identifiable like a relative location in a locational space by means of mutual determination aided by positions and distances, but is clearly determined in the environment in itself. An example of this can be found in the skilful evasion of an impending mass despite lacking information about position and distance, as discussed in the third hour. Then one's own felt body, the location of which essentially overlaps with one's own material body, is found in an absolute location and is set in relation to an object by means of a system of irreversible directions, partly by emitting glances, partly by the suggestion of motion of the impending object. There clearly is motion in surfaceless spaces, but there is also rest, for instance, in festive silence and in water experienced as gently supporting. And this kind of rest has to be known already in order to say what a relative place and rest as remaining at it is.

The Space of one's own felt body is also surfaceless, in contrast to the space of one's own material body that is represented by the perceptual body schema with positions and distances. In no stirrings of the felt body are surfaces to be noticed, neither in pain, hunger, lust etc. nor in the embodied involvement with emotions, for instance in being angry or joyful. For this reason, the felt body is not delimited and is not three-dimensional; it cannot be sliced by surfaces and is, in this sense, indivisibly extended, however, not without being spatially structured. Stirrings of the felt body partly take hold of it holistically like the more or less energetic or dull and then changeable feeling right after getting up in the morning, partly they do so in a partial manner and are then spread out over islands of the felt body. For most of the time the felt body is a swaying of diffuse islands, of which one can convince oneself if one discounts the testimony of the five senses and the perceptual body schema. Such an island is regularly formed in the vital drive in the regions of the abdomen or the chest when breathing in, where initially the swelling predominates and gradually becomes tension until its predominance, before becoming unbearable, by breathing out is released into privative expansion. Other fairly constant islands of the felt body are found in the oral and anal regions as well as in the soles of the feet. Otherwise, the islands of the felt body come and go; they become obtrusive, for instance, in head-, tooth- or stomachaches, and recede into the background again.

Individual islands of the felt body, too, have absolute locations. Let me elaborate on this by taking the example of an insect bite. When a sting or an itch seems to indicate an unwanted visitor, the dominant hand immediately moves to the irritated spot in order to get rid of or crush the troublemaker. It needs not be sought in a relative location by determination of their position and distance to certain body parts, it immediately reaches where it is needed, even though the relevant spot has not yet been identified in the perceptual body schema. Both partners in intracorporeal communication, the hand and the island formed by the irritation are accessible in the body's motor schema as absolute locations from a source of reference not determined in a relative-locational manner via irreversible directions. Thus, they can connect with each other irrespective of positions and distances. This example shows how strong the cohesion in the unity of the felt body is despite being spread out over islands. This unity is sustained by the contracting component of the vital drive, which thus has a dual role: as the opponent of expansion (tension vs. swelling) and as integrator (connector) of islands to the unity of the felt body. For this reason the degree of the unfolding of islands of the felt body is tied to the weight of contraction in the vital drive. So if contraction becomes weaker, the connection is loosened and the islands of the felt body flourish in a richer and easier manner, for instance, in sunbathing on the grass or by the beach, in the relaxation of autogenic training; but as soon as privative expansion becomes isolated from the vital drive and the protopathic tendency floods the felt body, the islands are molten and disappear more and more. If, on the other hand, tension strongly increases, the islands of the felt body shrink and also disappear, but this time through contraction and not expansion. Then the felt body can feel empty from fear or hunger. The connection of the formation as well as the shrinking of islands of the felt body with contraction and expansion can also be used therapeutically, not only in elaborate relaxation techniques but also in naïve interpersonal attending to one another. In an untitled poem with the first line "Why did you give us those deep glances?", Goethe praises the effect of Ms. Stein on him:

And in your angelic arms rested
The destroyed heart itself up again[3]

The strange (phrasal) verb "rest up" brings together in one term the flourishing of islands of the felt body in the region of the chest with the relaxing and calming expansion of the felt body.

Furthermore, emotions as atmospheres are spatial in a surfaceless space. An *atmosphere* in the sense meant here is the unbounded occupation of a surfaceless space in the region of what is experienced as present. (I say "occupation" and not "satisfaction", because one can also be dealing with an occupation with emptiness, as I will illustrate in what follows.) Claiming the spatiality of emotions is a tough and almost incredible challenge, as emotions are commonly construed as private states of the soul. This conception is the result of the psychologistic-reductionist-introjectionist objectification; but shortly before this shift, Empedocles construed love and anger (conflict) differently, that is, as spatially extended atmospheres – "balanced in all directions", equal in length and width" – which are implanted into the limbs of mortals, i.e. which corporeally possess them[4]. For the early Christians the Holy Ghost was just such an atmosphere in which they lived, of love, joy and freedom; for Paul it was

---

3   Translation by R. O. Müllan.
4   Freeman (1948, 31B17, lines 19-24).

a force keeping the felt body possessed in competition with an opponent, the flesh closely akin to Empedocles' anger-conflict. The foundational pillar of the psychologistic-reductionist-introjectionist objectification is psychologism, the act of locking the entirety of personal experience into a closed-off private inner sphere, a soul; after having done away with it in the third hour, introjection, too, becomes superfluous, as the inner, into which the content of the world could be fobbed off, is no longer at one's disposal. As soon as one has convinced oneself, the new view of emotions as bodily moving forces poured out spatially becomes quite natural. Here one can see how artificial the conception of emotions as states of the soul, as "passiones animae" (Thomas of Aquinas, building on Aristotle) is, for instance, in the case of anger. Much rather, it is experienced in the manner of a sense of an overpowering gravity, when one trips and only catches one's balance at the last minute, often like a force suddenly overcoming the felt body and dragging it forward or down, in contrast to the sense of gravity the downward tendency of which one opposes, rather, as force with which one goes along, at least to some extent out of an impulse of one's own until the personal conflict with the impulse taking hold of one then possibly sets in in succumbing and/or in resistance. Using a series of emotions, I now want to illustrate how much more apt a conception of them as atmospheres is than as states of the soul.

Festive seriousness is a powerful emotion which, as an atmosphere, presents itself mainly in the form of a wide, calm and densely gathered silence, with an authority that prohibits boisterous chatter. This emotion is free of pleasure or displeasure; the common interpretation of emotions as forms of pleasure and displeasure is refuted by this counterexample.

Joy is an uplifting atmosphere which causes the felt body to levitate ("in bliss"), to assume a springy step, even to jump ("for joy"), even though nothing changes about the body's gravity; but it no longer makes an impression as an obstacle. This could be due to an enhanced sense of corporeal strength; but there is also a passive joy into which one falls relaxedly, for instance, when relieved of a burdensome worry. This joy lifts up no less than the corporeally active one. Then it can only be the atmosphere of joy the uplifting tendency of which, in contrast to earthen gravity, makes life light.

With shame it occasionally happens that someone behaves shamefully but is not themselves ashamed while those present and those belonging to them feel embarrassed. Emotional contagion is out of the question here, for there is no one who could infect others with their shame. Much rather, shame here turns out to be an atmosphere which, from its densest region, the shamed person, whether feeling ashamed or not, radiates into the region of felt presence or beyond it, whereas it gets weaker towards the fringes, becomes a mere embarrassment, by which one is only touched but not thoroughly gripped. Someone who is merely embarrassed does not, like someone in the grip of catastrophical shame, want to disappear in the ground but would rather be gone; he does not lower his gaze but maybe squints his eyes a bit in order not to see things too precisely. But this embarrassment is just a watered-down version of the shame that hits him, who is at its densest region, catastrophically; this can be seen in the fact that this catastrophical shame, too, occurs as embarrassment. In such cases one says: "I am terribly embarrassed that…"

Sadness/grief is an area of experienced presence of an extended atmosphere with a total claim of assertion. Let me illustrate this by what I call the social emotional contrast. For this purpose, I compare two emotions, sadness and joy, with two kinds of embodied stirrings of the felt body that are closely related to them, fatigue and freshness; sadness tends to go hand in hand with fatigue and joy with freshness. When a joyful person with some degree of sensitivity surprisingly encounters a group of grieving people, he will somewhat dampen the expression of his joy to, at least, a touch of shy reserve. If, however, such a person encounters merely fatigued people, he will not, even with sensitivity, feel called upon to show such reserve; if he wants something from them, he will rather tend to shake them up by calls or by physical action, to offer them something strengthening or to send them to the doctor or get one for them. My question now is on what this difference in the degree of contrast is based. One could think that it is respect for the grieving people and their human dignity. But such respect would rather be a motive to pick those grieving up in order to give them back the upright posture of pride and dignity. Also this motive could not explain the contrast, since the fatigued persons have the same rightful claim to dignity. Much rather, it is the authority of the sadness as an atmosphere which completely and exclusively claims the space of felt presence and by the gravity of its authority more or less suppresses the atmosphere of joy that would otherwise also claim the space of felt presence. Emotions have authority, as has already been seen in the case of festive seriousness; if in a space of felt presence contrasting emotions noticeably collide, only the atmosphere with higher authority wins out, but only in the felt experience of a person receptive to the conflict. Mere embodied stirrings such as fatigue, freshness and a feeling of comfort while lying in a bathtub are no such spatially extended atmospheres and have no authority. As such, the contrast between fatigue and freshness does not inhibit persons affected as much as the contrast between joy and sadness/grief.

Here, desperation is not to be taken in the sense of a cancellation of desires and needs, but rather as the acedia of the Christian Desert Fathers of late antiquity who, as hermits in the noon day heat, could no longer find any purpose and, like the ennui of the French, a kind of boredom intermingled with nausea/disgust. It is an emotion which has a lot in common with sadness/grief, for instance, the sluggishness, the faint-heartedness and the tendency towards isolating oneself, but is different from it in that it is not depressing but rather brings with it an instability, an exposure to an atmosphere of intrusively felt emptiness in which no direction is sketched, not even of depressing grief which causes one to cower. This emotion, which in virtue of the instability it brings about causes a restlessness without direction, can be instilled by reflecting on the pointlessness of life, but also spontaneously overcome a human as a gripping atmosphere. This is the case, for instance, in the eerie mood of the evening when the pale coolness of the fading day makes everything appear distant, as if it were under a bell jar, and imbues it with a sense of alienness so that the directions of embodied attentiveness no longer find an anchor and a grip. Then the impression of the pointlessness of life encroaches, even without being brought about as pondersome thought by the atmosphere of felt emptiness. Nietzsche describes this experience of the dawn in a gripping manner[5] but neglects that it is a grief, just as medieval theology, for instance, Aquinus, who no longer recognised acedia as spontaneous despair and confused it with symptoms such as laziness or similar ones such as grief/sadness. A wet and cold morning in an ugly sea of houses or at a railway station is a further example of an environment prone to bringing about such a feeling of pointlessness. The spatiality of the gripping atmosphere is then evident in feeling of the pervasively poured out emptiness (despite the presence of bodies in the environment).

Affective involvement always has the gestalt of an embodied stirring and sometimes is the involvement in emotions which grip the felt body by affecting the vital drive. But one should not confuse the gripping

---

5   Nietzsche (1950, 118).

atmosphere as an emotion with (emotional) feeling as being in the grip of an emotion. For there is also another kind of feeling, the mere perception of the atmosphere without being in the grip of it; sometimes the transition from this perception to being affectively involved occurs so smoothly that the gripping power in causing this involvement can be clearly traced. In this manner Goethe's Faust is involved when he enters Gretchen's chamber as a lustful spy:

What a feeling of peace, order, and contentment breathes round[6]!

The emotion in which he enters the chamber is opposed to this atmosphere, but obviously he is touched by it. An angry or malign person entering a church can make a similar experience and be persuaded by the mild, pious and festive atmosphere of its interior. In other cases, an atmosphere does not itself grip someone but in a mediated manner with an opposing emotion, for instance, if a serious observer of a ludicrous festivity is thrown into a melancholy emotion by means of the atmosphere of ludicrous joy which he experiences as an incursion. It can even happen that an emotion as an atmosphere lies in the air without anyone feeling it (being in the grip of it) and grips a person in a mediated manner in virtue of a pre-emotion they feel. This is the case in non-personal anger that, in a mediated manner, haunts a person tormented by grave guilt under the guise of fear. The matricidal Orestes shows this kind of involvement in Aeschylus's tragedy before the appearance of the Erinyes:

> Hear! I know not the end; I am as one,
> Whose horses whirl his car without the course,
> Swept helpless in the tumult of my brain.
> There is some terror at my heart, that hums
> A jangling strain, a fierce delirious reel.[7]

In Goethe's Faust, Gretchen, having murdered her child, is tormented by grave guilt and in the cathedral hears the voice of a hallucinated evil spirit who kindles the fear of her conscience: "Horror seizes thee!"[8] But this anger lacks a person who is angry; it is a naked atmosphere, carried out in gripping fear. So the affective involvement in an emotion is second to the gripping effect of an emotion as an atmosphere.

---

6   Goethe (1908, 79).
7   Aeschylus (1900, 80, lines 1021-1025).
8   Goethe, *Faust*, p. 118.

But one has to be careful not to reify emotions as though they always hovered in space like invisible clouds. Emotions are half-things/entities. Half-things differ from full-things with regard to two properties. 1. Their duration can be interrupted, that is, they come and go, without there being any point in asking what they did in the meantime. 2. Whereas causality generally is tripartite, subdivided into cause (e.g. a falling stone), influence (e.g. impact) and effect (e.g. the destruction or dislodgement of the object hit), the causality of half-things is bipartite and immediate in that cause and influence overlap. A typical example is the voice of a human which one throughout all its sonic permutations hears as the same voice; the sonic wave may increase, the voice, however, does not. If it falls silent, it is pointless to start looking for it and how it passes its interruptions. As a physical object, the voice takes effect via several intermediate stages of influence, for instance, sonic waves, electric currents in the neurons, but these are constructions which only have their credibility in virtue of successful prediction, they are no facts of spontaneous life experience that would have to be considered as phenomena. Seen as a phenomenon, a voice immediately takes effect, just like a gaze by which one is hit, not by intermediate stages of influence. Other half-things are the wind (before being re-interpreted as air in motion, a "Vollding" [full-thing]), an overpowering sense of gravity as when one slips and only catches his balance at the last minute, an electrical shock (into which physics reads electricity as a hitting arm in order to complete the causality into the tripartite one of full-things), the pain with which one has to deal (III), many noises which become unbearable when stretched out (e.g. shrieking whistles), melodies, rhythms, night and also time when it becomes unbearable in boredom and tense expectation.

Emotions, too, are half-things. An emotion of bitterness, for instance, suddenly arises, takes hold of the embittered person and disappears until it returns after an unpredictable period of time and immediately, without interspersed influence, grips the person again. From the interruptibility of the duration of emotions results the impression that they are private. In this sense, they are like catchy melodies triggered by memories of one's own life story. As such, very personal idiosyncratic experiences and entanglements from one's life story conjure up the emotion like a melody stretched out over seemingly unconnected points in time and space, which is then only accessible to the person with the respective life story. But actually it is not the emotion that is private but the feeling of being in its grip, a fact subjective for the subject involved. However, emotions can be just as accessible individually (to each conscious subject) as collectively.

An example of such collective emotions were the waves of homesickness by which Russian refugees in the West were haunted after World War II[9]. Other examples are the inspired courage of an attacking and the panic of a fleeing troop.

Feeling an emotion as affective involvement is an embodied experience, in which an atmosphere grips the vital drive. Depending on the form of binding of contraction and expansion (tension and swelling) in it, differences in dispositions to being gripped result. Bathmothymics with a compact drive just like a long wind of vitality that builds up pressure only after having been heavily strained for too long and then suddenly effects a change in the level of the drive, are not as easily gripped as others, since their drive is not as easily stirred. People disposed to greater oscillations of tension and swelling or splitting parts of privative contraction and privative expansion from the whole complex resonate more easily with the gripping emotion. Other inhibitions or enhancements of the disposition to be gripped have personal reasons, for instance, in that the personally emancipated conscious subject only in doses admits embodied affective involvement, or in that a youth, from the not yet fully scaffolded elevation of his personal emancipation all too easily drifts off into being gripped, or because of fossilisations rooted in one's life story etc.

This form of being in the grip of an emotion differs from affective involvement without resonance with gripping emotions, for instance, pain, hunger, thirst, freshness and fatigue in that, from the word go, the person involved is more deeply entangled. The reason for this is that the affective involvement in emotions is only real if the person involved at least goes along a little with the emotions's impulse by spontaneously embracing it, whereas the conscious engagement with the emotion in terms of giving in or resisting only takes place later. I have already drawn attention to this in the case of anger. A symptom of this initial identification with the gripping emotion is marked clarity of gestural and facial expression. One has to be a very good actor indeed to adequately

---

9   Pfister-Ammende (1949, 253): "The waves of homesickness were strange. A Russian-speaking leader told us that during some evenings people stood up all of a sudden and, without any prior outward hint to this, silently went to their rooms where they sorrowfully yearned for their home country. A few hours or a day later this silent collective emotion was gone again. The leader said about this: 'I have never grasped how it is possible that all of a sudden all of them are stricken by the same feeling!'". Translation by Martin Bastert.

imitate the complex expression of joy. The laughing eyes, the springy step, the sunkenness in glee; a joyful person, no matter how clumsy, manages to do this effortlessly. Likewise, a downhearted person knows how to sigh and to assume a hunched position, an ashamed person how to lower their gaze, an angry person how to clench their fist, furrow their brow, intently stare etc. No one gripped in this manner needs to first ask how to do these things. However, someone feeling pity, who is not as thoroughly involved in someone else's pain as in their own, does often have to ask how to adequately express their pity. Only if this happens as spontaneously as if they were gripped by their own suffering, the expression is automatic. This naturalness of expression is the best evidence for the fact that a gripping emotion immediately affects the felt body with a suggestion of motion and the person gripped goes along with this by giving in to the emotion. Only a later personal stance can inhibit, suppress or enhance the expression by giving in to it. While being involved in mere embodied stirrings, the initial stance, having to deal with what brings about the involvement, is not wholly absent, but it does not so inevitably have the character of going along with or giving in to it. As such, it is much easier to observe a bodily stirring such as hunger or pain rather than a gripping emotion. With the latter, one has already identified before one begins to observe, even if, in subsequently taking a personal stance, one aims to reject or quell it. The entanglement and confrontation here is more intensive and dramatic than in the case of mere embodied stirrings, and, as such, it is much harder to observe it in an impartial manner.

The nature of the atmospheres that are emotions can be more precisely characterised by dividing emotions into three layers. The fundamental layer that is present in and colours all emotions, merely affects the expanse of surfaceless space. At this level, there are the alternatives of occupation by density or emptiness. The emotion of empty expanse is despair, as described earlier, in which anxiety and lethargy intermingle in a seemingly paradoxical manner due to the directionlessness and instability caused by the emptiness. The opposite is contentment, not as the gratification of desire but as an emotion of a dense and supporting expanse, most clearly felt as the emotion of warmth and security in the arms of a loved one or a family circle, but also in calm, composed and determined self-confidence and in the deep oceanic feeling that is the ideal of mysticism. Hegel talks about such a feeling when he writes to his wife: "There is a joyous contentment, which, seen without deception, is more than anything that is called happy."[10] All emotions are moods; contentment and despair are the pure moods. In their expanse a second layer of directed emotions is etched, pure excitements which are not centered on topics. Joy and sadness can be such uncentered excitements with elevating or supressing directionality; a classic formulation of this purity is found in Mörike's confession in his poem "*Verborgenheit*" [Concealment]:

> What I am sad about I know not,
> It is unknown woe;
> Always through tears I see
> The sun's loving light
>
> Often I am hardly self-aware,
> And the bright joy cajoles
> Through the gravity
> Which presses me in my breast.[11]

While such joy and sadness are directed (upward or downward) in a one-sided manner, worried anxiety as a vague sense of something eerie (e.g. in the woods at night) centripetally contracts around the person gripped; its opposite is a diffuse and aimless desire centrifugally drifting away in all directions, an emotion inherent in puberty and romance which was in detail studied by Goethe[12] and yet again classically exposed in Mörike's poem "*Im Frühling*" [In Spring]. A mixture of both emotions, centrifugal-centripetal to all directions is the emotion of the expectancy of a prescient person made topical by authors such as Goethe, Hölderlin and Hoffmann and in which an amalgam of something obscurely meaningful, threateningly and promisingly at same time, lies in the air[13]. The psychotic mood of beginning schizophrenia is of this kind.

Aimless pure excitements often – but with gradual transitions[14] – are grouped around a thematic centre and then become the transitive emotions directed toward objects which are ordinarily the prime examples of "emotions". The older school of phenomenology spoke of intentional emotions or emotions as intentional acts and so modelled their understanding

---

10   Hegel (1952, 367; letter from Hegel to Marie von Tucher, written in the summer
      of 1811). Translation by R. O. Müllan.
11   Translation by R. O. Müllan.
12   On this topic see Schmitz (1959, 254-263).
13   Schmitz (1969, 300-304).
14   Ibid. (324-330).

of emotions on "intending something"; accordingly, Franz Brentano, the originator of this interpretation, subsumed them, altogether with desires, under emotional acts and acts of will. This was a mistake in which one too lightly simply spoke of an (intentional) object of emotion. For, in most cases, this object has a dual character which can be described in the terms of gestalt psychology. Accordingly, I rather take the so-called intentional emotions to be gestalts which are thematically centered atmospheres than as centered emotions (excitements). The gestalt psychologist Wolfgang Metzger, in the case of optical gestalts, distinguished a dense region (where its characteristic features are gathered) and an anchoring point (from which the gestalt establishes itself)[15]. I have transposed this terminology to centered emotions. There is joy in something (the region of density), for instance, in seeing the beautiful landscape, and joy about something (the anchoring point), for instance, about success. There are also cases of joy in and about something, for instance, healthy and successful children; how these two can differ can be seen in the case of joy with regard to an examination: only if the course of the examination was joyful, the candidate had joy in the examination, otherwise only about passing it. In anger, the anchoring point is what one is angry about and the region of density is the person one is angry about. The region of density in the case of shame is the person shamed who, however, not always has to feel ashamed. The anchoring point here is the shaming flaw. In fear of a murderer, the region of density is the murderer and the anchoring point death. In the Western history of love a turning point is marked by the ejection of the anchoring point from the thematic centre of love. Classical philosophers had called for such an anchoring point and medieval "Minnesang" [courtly song] still relies on it in that the beauty, virtue and decency of the loved one were the anchoring points of love. Gottfried von Straßburg, in his *Tristan*, clearly amputates the anchoring point and this pioneering foray becomes the dominant paradigm for the modern romantic novel and even love life[16].

Freeing emotions from the introjection into the soul as proposed is of great importance, since law, morality and religion are based on the authority of emotions and for which mere private emotions in the souls of individual humans would be insufficient. *Authority* for someone is the property of being a power (i.e. an entity with executive control) by means of which the binding validity of norms is imposed in a clearly noticeable manner. A *norm*

---

15   Metzger (1975, 178 f., 181-183).
16   Schmitz (1993, 163-169, 179-195).

is a programme for possible obedience. A norm is *valid in a binding manner* for someone if they can only refuse their obedience to it in a half-hearted and biased manner. For them, it is *valid in a non-binding manner* if its validity is up to them, for instance, in the case of the rules of a game or of target arbitrarily set by themselves. The validity of a norm is doubly relative, first, with respect to a perspective and, second, with respect to an audience which can be much greater than the number of those who have the perspective. In the perspective of decent people, for all people as addressees, the norm holds that they should be decent. For a devoted member of a missionary religion, in their perspective, the binding norm holds that all should believe in their way. But this does not hold in the perspective of non-believers. The word "for" in "is valid for" is ambiguous in this sense.

Emotions have an authority, as I have borne out using examples such as festive seriousness, shame and grief/sadness. In the same manner, anger demands retribution with an authority the impact of which Kleist has aptly described in the character of Michael Kohlhaas. Respect demands restraint despite and with attention and deep joy demands gratitude (possibly not directed at anybody). Apart from emotion, evidence or, much rather, being, also have authority in that in evidence the latter is foregrounded as authority, which can, of course, only be recognised as being, since the person affected is already aquainted with it from the primitive present[17]. In evidence, being demands of the person affected to take themselves as someone confinced by the evident fact[18].

The binding validity of legal, moral and religious norms is based solely on the authority of emotions. In their stead, only coercion and convention might be considered as alternatives, but coercion needs no obedience and convention without the supporting authority of an emotion is merely sufficient for non-binding validity. In the case of law, anger and shame are the emotions that give it its pathos; without this pathos, law would become a whore in that any arbitrary system of norms could be passed off as law, no matter how despicable its content is. Anger and shame are centered emotions which enter through their anchoring point and, as cathartic excitements, strive to be released and cancelled by means of a reaction directed at their region of density. There are legal cultures of anger which prioritise subjective rights (in the West) and legal cultures of shame which

---

17   See Schmitz (1994, 243-247).
18   Schmitz (2012, 24-41).

subjugate subjective rights to the shaming of the person committing an offense (in East Asia and partially also in ancient Rome)[19]. The distinction is of a different kind than the by now popular one between cultures of shame and cultures of guilt, as Ruth Benedict has called them. Also, despite the priority of subjective rights in anger-based legal cultures, it is not the case that anger is merely indignation at the violation of one's rights. A simple counterexample is provided by the case of the piano teacher who is angry because his untalented pupil fails to play properly, because in his eyes, the dignity of the music and not his own rights are violated.

Anger and shame become *legal* when they exceed tolerable limits. Whether this is the case cannot, in a legal culture with a plurality of participants, be determined individually based on private judgements, for these are too variegated. Much rather, anger and shame have to enter into a jointly occurrent situation of the legal community, the content of which in terms of programmes which are norms – what I call the *Nomos* of this situation – determines when the level of what is bearable has been exceeded. This Nomos is not directly dictated by anger and shame but by the authority of emotional dispositions towards a sense of rights which is formed by dealing with wrongs. *Wrongs* are the anchoring points of legal anger (legal shame). The emotional sense of right and wrong ensures that the authoritative and thus 'sacred' but dangerous emotions anger and shame do not take such a form that one wrong leads to another, for instance, in the form of continued revenge. One can compare this emotional sense of right and wrong to respect. It would be indignating and shaming to come too close to or carelessly pass over what demands respect. Thus, respect is a precursor emotion of anger and shame. The same holds for the emotional sense of right and wrong, only with the difference that respect is thematically centred (in what is respected as the region of density and its awe-inspiring properties as anchoring point), but as a pure excitement it remains open to everything. Such an emotional sense of right and wrong is inscribed in the jointly occurrent situation of a legal people in the same manner that love is in the joint situation of lovers or a harmonious family and, as a half-thing, it can always be triggered in its members, without there being any point in asking how it passed the meantime and bridged the space-in-between.

---

19   See Schmitz (1973, 105-110; 1997, 153-165). Concerning the legal cultures of shame see also Wlosok (1980, 84-100).

The occurrent joint situation of a legal conviction supported by an emotional sense of right and wrong demarcates a *legal state* which is spared unbearable outbreaks of anger and shame, even if this goal is not reached and the legal state remains an ideal. A *right* is a *culture of law* consisting of a *legal people* and a *legal order* which is oriented towards a legal state determined by the emotional sense of right and wrong. For a legal people, in the borderline case of dealing with right and wrong for an individual conscience, a single member is sufficient. A legal people with a plurality of members needs a core group for whose members the emotional sense of right and wrong has authority; to this usually belongs an inner fringe group of conformists, for instance, opportunists, in whose perspective the legal order holds only in a non-binding manner, and an outer fringe group of humans (e.g. infants) to which it is merely applied. The *legal order* of a legal culture is the epitome of those norms that prescribe the actuality of the legal goods of this legal culture. *Legal goods* of a legal culture are the states of affairs, the actuality of which is essential for achieving and maintaining the legal order of this legal culture. The legal norms are partly core norms and partly peripheral norms. *Core norms*, in virtue of the emotional sense of right and wrong, are valid for the core group in a binding manner. Peripheral norms take effect if from the core norms a choice has to be made between a multitude of possible options, each of which is compatible with the core norms. In that case, the choice is left to a norm-giving institution, e.g. legislators in states or a patriarch in a patriarchal family. In this manner, the pathos of the law leaves a lot of leeway in a frame to be filled arbitrarily but suitably.

Morality is a special case of law. It is similar in that the binding validity of norms is based on the authority of anger and shame, to which is added a feeling of guilt though, which lies between shame and sadness/ grief. The atmosphere of shame, as I have described it[20], arises when a provocation, which can be a mere claim to validity, bounces off a resistance with the consequence that the embodied directions irreversibly leading from contraction to expansion are inhibited by an overpowering force of opposed centripetal vectors of emotion, which can be sensually embodied by the gazes directed at the person shamed, that the person gripped by shame can no longer unfold in an embodied manner, lowers their gaze and wants to crawl into a hole in the ground. Such inhibition of embodied directionality is also part of the emotion of guilt but under the influence

---

20   Schmitz (1973, 35-43).

of atmospherical vectors which are depressing rather than centripetal, in which way the emotion of guilt becomes similar to that of sorrow. But in contrast to sorrow which is depressing in a diffuse and divergent manner, a feeling of guilt encroaches on the person affected in a bodily pressing manner; thus, being in its grip, just as in that of shame, is imbued with a grinding and destructive forcefulness, which is lacking in being in the grip of sorrow.

Morality differs from law by an intensification of the authority of emotions into unconditional seriousness. The seriousness of an authority and of the bindingness of norms provided by it is determined by levels of personal emancipation. I will introduce this term in the next hour and, for the time being, leave it at saying that it is something like a capacity for critique. A person can, at the same time, be at more than one level of personal emancipation. A bindingness is of *limited seriousness* if it occurs at a level of personal emancipation above which there is yet a higher one. I clarify this, without yet defining the notion of 'height' of a level, by using the example of the shame which arises when one has embarrassed oneself, that is, has to take back a claim of validity. One can feel very ashamed even though one does not value society very much, that is, one can distance oneself, but nonetheless one cannot leave the lower level. The case is similar if one sticks with a tradition towards which one already takes a critical stance in reflection. But if, at the highest respectively achievable level of personal emancipation and in mobilising all resources of one's capacity for critique, one cannot refuse one's preparedness for obedience without doing so in a half-hearted and biased manner, then the bindingness of this norm and the authority by which it is provided is *unconditionally serious*. Unconditional seriousness is what the norm appearing in evidence has and which urges the person affected to admit a fact. The bindingness of a norm provided by the authority of anger, shame and/or a feeling of guilt is *moral* if it is unconditionally serious for someone. From this it follows that the unconditional bindingness of moral norms is relative to individual perspectives of particular persons and cannot be generalised at will. It depends on where the highest level of the capacity of critique lies and there is no reason to assume that it is the same for all persons. It is not even certain that there is a highest level for each person. There can be people without a conscience who, in complete frivolousness, rise above any authority imposed by anger, shame and guilt. In the perspective of such people, no norms are morally valid, they can, however, be addressees of the validity of norms that are morally binding for other people and be treated accordingly.

Religion is related to morality. One can see morality as much as a special religion as as a special law. *Religion* is behaviour out of affectedness by the divine; the affectedness need not be immediate but can also be passed on by tradition and then possibly fade into a routine as a mere echo of original affectedness. What is *divine* for someone is rooted in the authority of an emotion which is unconditionally serious to them; what anger, shame and guilt are to morality, is, as the divine, extended to situationally embedded emotions, the nomos of which is valid in a binding manner for the person affected in virtue of these emotions. Such situations are often segmented but can be condensed in the image of a character which represents them like a poster into a meaningful impression, so that they assume a shape which one can more firmly accommodate than the segmented situation. Such a character which can be real or imagined is then a god of the respective divine. In this sense, Tersteegen confesses at the beginning of his song: "I pray to the power of love that is revealed in Jesus." What is divine for him is the love to which he prays and Jesus is the god in which it is revealed, i.e. becomes condensed to a meaningful impression. Correspondingly Apollo is the god of the Southern Light, a sacred emotional force[21] both with respect to its illuminating and benevolent powerfulness as well as with respect to its cruelty. God is always only a character in the perspective of a person for whom the authority of an emotion is unconditionally serious in virtue of being in its grip and this amounts to a subjective fact for the person affected. In this sense, every god is my or "your God"[22], as Luther says, which does not mean though that everyone could have their own household god and that a god is nothing other than this. Much rather, the breadth of the fact subjective for me that something is my God reaches far beyond myself and my private life. It is the tragedy of religion that what reaches beyond it is immune to neutralisation; the attempt to translate it into an objective fact leads to a metaphysical misconception. Monotheistic religions have fallen prey to such a misconception by postulating a highest being that is omnipotent, omniscient, absolutely good and just. If this were so, one could be certain that even without doing anything oneself, everything would be arranged in the best possible way. It would, however, remain an open question whether this being is a god, for this is a matter not of power, wisdom or benevolence, but of authority with unconditional seriousness. It can only become manifest in superiority over the respectively highest

---

21   Schmitz (1977, 124-128).
22   Luther (1908, 44).

attainable level of personal emancipation; thus, there is a god only for a grown-up or growing-up human, whereby growing up begins in early childhood already.

Something still needs to be said about surfaces. Surfaces are alien to the felt body. In one's own felt body, in the form of embodied stirrings, one cannot feel surfaces. Precisely for this reason surfaces are so important for elevating the person out of life in the primitive present. By horizontally opposing the gaze into the depth of space, they release one from embodied communication in gazing. They offer the gaze a background for tracking reversible connections between possible targets of the gaze. Such connections can already be made without surfaces, for instance, in constructing constellations in the stars without being exactly linear (without width), for lines without width only occur between surfaces (as sharp edges). As long as, for instance, no surface is available for the networks of reversible connections, their arrangement shifts with every changing act of attention; only by inscribing the networks in surfaces do they become invariant. Thus, the possibility of constructing a stable locational space is provided. The person gazing can conceive of themselves within this locational space as the surface, by crossing the line of the gaze, gives them the opportunity to reflect on the direction of the gaze which, as an embodied stirring, irreversibly leads from contractedness to expansion. By reversing this direction on the surface crossed, the inverted directionality reaches one's own felt and material body of the person gazing, so that they can be integrated into the network of locations in locational space. In this manner the perceptual body schema is pre-formed as well as the incorporation of one's own material body, and with it, more or less coextensively located, one's felt body, into an encompassing locational space. An emancipated person then projects themselves, as material and felt body, into a neutral system which they can encounter on their emancipated level, so to speak, see themselves with other eyes; if, however, they believed to have in this manner left life in the primitive present behind, they would be deluding themselves. Another opportunity for developing the perceptual body schema is touching the smooth surface of one's own body, for instance, with one's hands to ward off parasites; this might well have been the way people got to know their bodies before the introduction of civilised hygiene.

The Development of the Person Personal Emancipation and Personal
Regression; the Personal Situation; the Embodied Disposition; One's
Own and Other's Personal Worlds; Consciousness

As the primitive present unfolds in five dimensions, the person emerges
from the life in the present in virtue of two accomplishments:

1. The absolutely identical conscious subject, by means of a self-
ascription as an instance of a type, becomes a singular subject increasing
the number of subjects by 1.

2. In the life in the primitive present all meanings are subjective for
someone. By neutralising a part of them, something emerges that is alien to
the singular subject. Something is alien for someone in the sense intended
here if the state of affairs that it exists, whether factually true or not, is
encountered as a neutral (objective) state of affairs. Vis-a-vis the alien,
the person can take recourse to something of its own. Later it will be
characterised as a personal situation and as a personal world.

The interaction of both accomplishments, that is, of singularisation and
of neutralisation, can be observed in the exemplary case of disappointment.
In such a state, meanings that previously were a subtle part of the internally
diffuse meaningfulness of situations, are explicitly singled out as particular.
For instance, one notices how well one was off only in virtue of what,
in particular, is experienced as absent, in virtue of the programmes that
no longer work, in virtue of the problems that in disappointment are
experienced as singular. This also enriches self-ascription: the conscious
subject sees itself in new roles, as someone who has experienced loss and
as someone who copes, as an instance of a new genus. On the other hand,
for him, many meanings that are revealed to be illusory are stripped of
subjectivity and other states of affairs, programmes and problems, which
take their place, are neutral for the sobered-up subject and make alien what
was familiar. But not only what is immediately noticed becomes alien or
neutral. Since states of affairs are often genera with unfathomably many

cases[1], all these cases, be they meanings, be they things of other kinds, become alien according to these genera; an overarching neutralisation can, even without singularisation, drag a great mass down into neutrality. So for this reason all meanings, i.e. all facts, originally are subjective for someone; this results from the fact that the unfolded present (the world), by means of sentential speech, is emancipated from the life in the primitive present in which all meanings are subjective for someone. But by no means are all meanings individually subjective before they become objective, for in masses neutralisation precedes singularisation. So while objectivity or neutrality is a faded remainder of full-blooded subjectivity for someone, by no means each fact has to first have been subjective for someone to then become objective.

Instead of such de-valued meanings, disappointment presents new individual, hard facts with which one has to deal; in this way it demands accountability to oneself and thus self-ascription. Therefore, by combining individualisation and neutralisation, disappointment is an important step in maturation for humans; animals, too, can be disappointed, but, as it seems, they do not bring to it these two achievements, rather they remain caught in unexplicated situations. I have singled out disappointment, because it exemplarily illuminates the basic process of becoming a person; apart from it, many other paths lead to becoming a person for humans. On all these paths humans make valuable experiences for self-ascription that provide them with meanings (states of affairs, programmes, problems) subjective for them. These feed into the meanings taken over from the primitive present that have remained internally diffuse. Thus results a richer meaningfulness as the seed of the state-like personal situation which is the personality of a person. This *personal situation* changes over the course of a life story without end by means of processes of personal emancipation and personal regression, of explication and implication in view of challenges. I will elucidate these concepts.

Personal emancipation is the singularisation and neutralisation of meanings with the consequence that what is idiosyncratic can set itself off from what is neutral and alien and thus personality solidifies and develops. The ability of critiquing, the strategic overview for organising means to ends pursued and impartial evaluation are competencies of personal emancipation, which have incurred the unclear honorary title of reason,

---

1   See page 76, footnote 2.

however, one exposed by philosophers like Kant like a fetish. Depending on the distance to the life in the primitive present on which a person draws for its opportunity for self-ascription (III), levels of personal emancipation differ; according to the degree and extent of the neutralisation of meanings, the higher level is the one more neutralised. A person can, at the same time, be at many different levels of personal emancipation. One example of this, the authority of emotions with limited seriousness, was brought up in the previous hour. A further example is akrasia which is introduced to the philosophical debate by Aristotle in the 7th book of the *Nicomachean Ethics*. In anglo-saxon analytic philosophy and its sphere of influence it has recently been much debated but misleadingly been equated with the term 'weakness of will'. The case is that a person forms two incompatible intentions at different levels of personal emancipation. While he favours the one at the higher level, the one capable of critique, because this intention is more easily justified, he actually chooses the one formed at the lower level, because it is more richly invested in the subjectivity of affective involvement. An example is the lazy bed-dweller, who, with good reasons, due to important tasks at hand, justifies getting up immediately after waking but finds his bed so comfortable that he chooses the intention to remain lying in bed. This is not a case of weakness of will, for an intention is not just formed but also enacted; here we are not dealing with a weak but with a complex will.

For having the relatum of self-ascription, a person needs access to the primitive present and thus, counter to its personal emancipation, has to dive back into life in the primitive present where, by means of the vital drive and embodied affective involvement, he has access to the primitive present (III). This is the achievement of *personal regression* which serves personal re-subjectification as much as personal emancipation serves neutralisation. By using the qualifier 'personal' I wish to indicate that this direction of the process is just as necessary as the ascent to neutrality and impartial factuality in personal emancipation. Both processes, emancipation and regression, explicate and implicate; they explicate individual meanings from the personal situation and implicatingly let them fall back into their internally diffuse meaningfulness. Personal emancipation explicates by singularisation according to its concept and implicates by indifferently degrading and passing over many things in neutralising; personal regression implicates, because the life in the primitive present, into or close to which it falls back, does not know the form of individualisation, but it also explicates by confronting humans with something around which there is no way. An important, even necessary contribution to the development of the personal situation by means of the implication of individual meanings into their internally diffuse meaningfulness is achieved by forgetting. Without forgetting, the personal situation could not develop any further; it would fall apart into several chunks of individual experiences.

The interaction of personal emancipation and personal regression can be studied in cases of laughing and crying. Laughing is falling from a level of personal emancipation into life in the primitive present in the confidence of being able to return to this level, because the energy of personal regression is sufficient for this; as such it is akin to a circle on the beam. The comic nature of the situation additionally ensures this confidence by a reduplication of the level of personal emancipation into one prone to regression of what is laughed at and one kept in reserve with integrity of laughing; when what is laughed at is identical with whom is laughing, the comic situation becomes humour. So who is laughing regresses and, at the same time, in their confidence of returning instantiates a triumph over personal regression. Crying, on the other hand, sets in if the person cannot remain at a level of personal emancipation under encroaching pressure and so regresses into life in the primitive present, contracting under the encroaching pressure and closely scraping by the life in the primitive present, but in such a manner that the person in crying their heart out while scraping by finds an inkling of a new level of personal emancipation instead of returning to the old one. Both processes integrate the person by fusing personal emancipation with personal regression, but laughing leads no further, while crying gives a life story a chance of further development.

The person has an ambiguous relation to his personal situation. On the one hand, he cannot, against the developing backdrop of her life story, get rid of it. On the other, he is not as caught in it as in a soul, but he also lives pre-personally in the primitive present, not only in states of shock or bewilderment, in laughing or crying, but in all spontaneous motor enaction, for instance, in chewing food which, in the case of persons, is not enacted differently than in the case of animals. A good example for the person's intermediary position between the life in the primitive present and the unfolded present by means of singularisation is speech. On the one hand, it leads to singularisation by means of the explication in sentential speech of the meanings of situations. On the other, the speaker takes the lead for his speech as an internally diffuse holistic situation from programmes or recipes for the presentation of states of affairs, programmes and/or problems, i.e. from sentences. He deals with them as routinely as with his movable limbs, for instance, his mouth in carelessly chewing food: he does not, first of all, take account of the stock of programmes, but, as a competent speaker, blindly selects sentences that fit his presentational intentions only by individually explicating them in speaking. So in relation to his fluent speech the speaker lives in the primitive present, but in relation to what he speaks about, i.e. the meanings presented in his speech, he lives in the unfolded present.

The person does not only – by means of personal regression and in spontaneous routines – live in his personal situation but is also faced with it vis-a-vis like a partner, even an oracle of which he has to make sense. This is most clearly seen in the case of difficult life choices. In such cases, a pondering back and forth sets in which does not serve the purpose of goal-directed reasoning but is rather a playing-through of the personal situation that tries to extract from it what fits it in view of the alternative to be decided upon. When this becomes clear, the decision has been made and reasoning is aborted. A nice example of such a process is provided by the report the mathematician Hermann Weyl gives of how, from his position in Zurich, he decided to reject the prestigious offer from the university of Göttingen as the successor of the famous Felix Klein: "when the decision could no longer be postponed, for hours I ran around a block of houses debating the matter with my wife and finally jumped aboard a late tram calling to her: 'But there is no other option than to accept.' But then I must have noticed the cheerful bustle that was unfolding on and around the lake on this pleasant summer evening: I went to the counter and sent a telegraph with my rejection. Of course, my wife was surprised when I came home."[2] In a less dramatic manner, each act of willing, also in banal contexts, is of this kind. It consists of the two phases of forming and realising the intention. The forming of an intention happens in light of a challenge in questioning the personal situation, perhaps with the aid of diplomatic mediation of divergent tendencies in it. In this phase, willing is a feat of intelligence leading to knowledge of what one wants, i.e. of what is fitting in one's personal situation. The matter is the same in choosing from a menu in a restaurant. The personal situation is here unnoticeably engaged by the subtle meaningfulness of the synaesthetic characters invested in the offered meals which are bridging qualities of embodied communication, that is,

---

2   Weyl (1968, 650). Rich material of similar content can be found in Thomae (1960).

they can be felt corporeally (III). Sartre has attempted to bring out such subtle meaningfulness using the example of stickiness, especially sugary stickiness[3]. Successful intention formation is followed by realisation in the form of the involvement of the vital drive. In both phases, willing can misfire. But if it succeeds, successful willing already amounts to action, independent of whether a movement of the body is intended and then is enacted. Calculating is an action just as jumping.

Partly the personal situation is deeply embedded in shared situations and partly it is loosely incorporated into them and contains many partial situations which glide and rub against each other like thick liquids in another thick liquid. Such partial situations are partly retrospective like the crystallised centres of memory and partly presentist like the standpoints of a person, the composure that he loses when he loses his temper, his attitude (as a way of permitting affective involvement), his techniques of living (as a way of dealing with problems of how he lives his life), his vocabulary, his habitual interests; partly they are prospective as forward-looking scripts, what the person is aiming at and what he wishes to avoid. These prospective partial situations are often very difficult for him to access and intensively interact with the retrospective ones.

The personal situation is given a foundation, like the higher voice ranges by the bass in an orchestra, in a personal embodied disposition which decides how the vital drive can be used and which preconditions exist, apart from the specifically personal ones, for openness, for resonance with moving emotions. While also the protopathic and the epicritcal as well as the embodied direction which irreversibly leads from contractedness to expansion are co-determining factors for the embodied disposition, what is always most significant is the strength and form of binding of the vital drive. A weak drive hinders the integrating incorporation of episodes of life experience into the personal situation; as such, the personality is not rounded off. If sufficiently strong, the form of binding of the two components contraction and expansion can vary in three respects, which I have marked with the terms for types coined by Kretschmer and Veit which I have re-interpreted to denote differences in embodied dispositions. In compact binding, in which (acutely, as in pain and breathing in, lifting and pulling) tension and swelling are thickly interconnected, receptivity is rather dull, but robustness is great, though without any chance of elastic

---

3   Sartre (1943, 690-708: De la Qualité comme Révélance de l'Etre).

evasion as a means of compensating strain; as such, they build up after too much intensity or duration, and the build-up can only be released by a sudden change of the level of the drive upward (explosion in the extreme) or downward (until breaking down). This is how the type of the bathmothymic, as Veit calls him, results. Veit further subdivides this type into phlegmatics who are difficult to set in motion and dynamicists who are difficult to calm down; in the former case there is an overweight of tension in the compact vital drive, in the latter of swelling. The embodied disposition of the cyclothymic, however, is capable of rhythmical oscillation and, as such, easily resonates with emotional upheavals. The vital drive of the schizothymic, whose embodied disposition favours splitting privative contraction from tension and privative expansion from swelling, is capable of resonating, not by means of the rhythmical ebb and flow of expansion and contraction but by splitting. On the one hand, it can be driven into a contracted state, be intimidated, devastated, imposed upon by worries or, on the other, it can take off in a light and invigorated manner; the schizothymic compensates this instability by means of the licence of privative expansion to overstep the contracted confines of the felt body and in personal emancipation ironically or strategically transcend the situation. This may happen circuitously, but it is a means of staying on track. What is more noteworthy than the personal embodied dispositions are those which are collectively prevalent among populations in certain eras. One can almost physically sense their changes when one compares the nervous and overly tense age of powerlessness, of trembling, of great visions and deliria from Richard Wagner to Hitler with the subsequent age (up to now) of robust, but numb vitality receptive only to strong and coarse stimuli: a schizothymic and a bathmothymic disposition. This change of collectively dominant embodied dispositions also affects the change in artistic style[4].

The personal situation consists mainly of meanings (states of affairs, programmes, problems and their internally diffuse complexes). But what is idiosyncratic to a person fills a whole further sphere, to which everything belongs on which they depend in affective involvement, be it friendly or hostile. I aim to get a grip on this further sphere by the notion of a 'personal idiosyncratic world' within the personal world. The personal world of a person consists of their personal idiosyncratic world and their personal alien world. To the *personal idiosyncratic world* of a person belong all meanings which are subjective for him and everything for which the (factual or non-

---

4   See Schmitz (2008b, 317-352); see also Schmitz (1966, 257-298; 2011, 113-120).

factual) state of affairs that they exist is of this kind. To the *personal alien world* belong all meanings which have lost subjectivity for him by means of neutralisation (i.e. objectivisation) and everything for which the (factual or non-factual) state of affairs that they exist is of this kind. (Non-factual states of affairs need to be taken into consideration, because many things, that do not actually exist, belong to the personal world of a person, for instance, things he hopes or fears in indulging in illusions.) According to the relation of personal idiosyncratic world and personal alien world three types of people can be distinguished: the extrovert, the introvert and the ultrovert. For the extrovert the line between both partial worlds is only finely drawn, that is, the alienness of the personal alien world is obfuscated. He is in danger, on the one hand, of becoming scattered, because he cannot retreat into the personal idiosyncratic world, on the other, of naively combining heroic commitment with an exaggerated claim to the world: because for his more or less everything he deals with is *his*, he is prepared to fight for them but also wants to possess them. For the introvert there is a clear dividing line between the personal idiosyncratic world and the personal alien world and his concern is directed primarily at the personal idiosyncratic world. He is in danger of becoming locked in too rigid a defensive stance at the endangered border of the two partial worlds, be this by walling himself off, which can appear dulled, or by retreat out of whiny hypersensitivity. In the case of the ultrovert, the line is just as clearly drawn as in the case of the introvert, but he transcends the personal idiosyncratic world (hence "ultro") in his care and commitment to the personal alien world, for instance, as a member of political or economic organisations which, for him, function as ends in themselves, or as a perfectionist superhumanly focussed on matters of fact in the roles of engineer, mathematician, scientist or doctor[5]. This is possible due to the vast grey areas in which the subjectivity of meanings fades into neutrality or objectivity. A slight touch of this shade of grey is already present in any statement about oneself. Who can at least still say "I am sad" is no longer as sad as someone who is dumbstruck. In many statements people

---

5   A typical ultrovert is the so-called (Saxon) 'Grundtoffel': "He seizes upon important and unimportant, purposeful and purposeless, everyday occurrence, specials and esoterism in the same dogged, stern manner, twists and turns it laboriously and gnarly, and during the period of his handy and intellectual >examination<, he does not see anything but the isolated, unrelated matter in question." "He is generally more interested in the tasks themselves than in his own accomplishments." "He commonly is uninteresting for himself." (Walter Beck in: *Menschenformen. Volkstümliche Typen*, edited by von Voß and Max Simoneit, Berlin: Bernard & Graefe, 1941, 88-91, as cited in Schmitz (1980, 406)).

make about themselves it is not easy to decide whether they are speaking whether they care about and are moved by what they say about themselves or whether they are speaking in a purely factual manner as of an object; in that case both attitudes fade into one another. For the ultrovert, so much subjectivity has already faded over, that he, without losing it, casts it into his personal alien world. He is in danger of not stopping at anything, not at the concerns of others whom he shifts off into his personal alien world, and not at his own affective involvement which, however, cannot really be killed off, since the ultrovert would then lose his own self-consciousness (with or without self-ascription) and thus would lose his personhood; the remainder rumbles in the personal idiosyncratic world and sometimes takes revenge by fading over into the personal alien world.

The personal situation replaces the closed-off private inner sphere of the psychologistic-reductionist-introjectionist objectification in all its forms, not just of the soul but also of consciousness, which, since Descartes, has been a competitor of the soul, and from Kant to Husserl and Sartre ascends to being its rightful heir. This is so influential that older phenomenology purports to be the analysis of consciousness oriented towards intentional acts allegedly found in consciousness. To this end, Husserl coined the slogan: "all consciousness is consciousness of something." In this formula the word is used ambiguously. In the first sense it denotes a collection of all contents of consciousness; Husserl mentions acts, hyletic data (i.e. sensations) and retentions (phases of experiences that have just passed). In the second sense it denotes the having-in-consciousness of the conscious subject who is conscious of something. In my opinion there is consciousness in the second sense, a having-in-consciousness, but not a consciousness in the first sense of an inner world. This is a strong claim which runs counter to many widely accepted truisms. I base it on an old argument for the simplicity of the conscious subject or, as I adapt it, of having-in-consciousness. We first encounter the argument in Plotin[6] with a particularly interesting earlier sketch in Aristotle[7] which concerns the evaluation of the difference in the data from various senses. Plotin, too, mentions the difference but foregrounds the perception of complexes. I will exclusively draw on relational consciousness. As an example I chose the idea of the similarity of the sun and the moon (as luminaries). It contains three linked ideas which nowhere overlap in the object; for nothing of the

---

6   Plotinus (*Enneads*, IV.7.6.1-34 (second treatise in chronological order)).
7   Aristotle (*De Anima*, 426b12-427a16).

similarity can be seen in the sun, nor can anything of the sun be seen in the moon etc. As such, no combination of the three component ideas can be adequate to the whole idea, as Kant – focussing on complexes rather than relation – claimed in his failed attempt at refutation by trying to compose the whole idea of a verse from the partial ideas of words just as he claimed that "the movement of a body is the united movement of all its parts"[8] If one combines the ideas of similarity, sun and moon, one gets three connected ideas with three separate objects but nothing of the similarity between the sun and the moon; while the having-in-consciousness of this similarity is founded on these partial ideas, it is not composed of them. From this follows the simplicity of having-in-consciousness of relations of any level of complexity. But this having-in-consciousness must be just as multiform as it is simple, for it contains the relation and all its places. How is this multitude compatible with simplicity[9]? This problem is the same as that with the Christian dogma of trinity, that more than one person, despite their differences, are supposed to be the same unitary god.

This riddle can only be resolved in the way it was done in the fourth hour with the Husserlian doll for time and suggested for antinomies. But the competition of different ways of having-in-consciousness for identity with the same thing is no source of confusing disconcertion, for other than in that case the competitors are not incompatible with one another. It only consists in the fact that the partial ideas, of which each one for itself is clearly distinguished from each other one, is so infinitely weakly distinguished in simple relational consciousness (more precisely: having-in-consciousness of the relation between them) that neither their identity nor their difference in the whole idea is clearly determined, nor undecidedness about it, nor distinction iterated finitely many times (in the sense that it is undecided whether it is undecided or that it is undecided that it is undecided that it is undecided etc.). In the grey area of infinite undecidedness all determinations fail. Much rather, there is a multitude of another type than the numerical multitude of individual things, a multitude which also cannot be attained by a synthetic unity and no composition; I speak of an unstable or ambivalent multitude, in which the simplicity of the whole and a multitude of the parts become compatible by means of the competition of the parts for identity with the whole. The having-in-consciousness of relations and even any sort of having-in-consciousness of singular things are of this kind (thing =

---

8   Kant (1998, 417 (A 353)).
9   Aristotle gave thought to a similar problem, see page 119, footnote 7.

something in general). Something is singular if it increases an amount by 1. The difference from a state reduced by 1 is contained in this idea. In so far every idea of a singular thing is a consciousness of relation[10].

It was a mistake of theorists of consciousness from Descartes to Husserl and their followers to assume a consciousness with a numerical multitude of many contents of consciousness and their arrangement[11] instead of an ambivalent multiform having-in-consciousness which, in infinite distinction between simplicity and multitude, very well is capable at the same time of having many topics or objects and of clearly distinguishing them. One has projected a model of bodies from the external world into an inner world which does not exist in this form, with several singular contents of consciousness as particles or figures in it, the mind which Hume compared with a theatre[12].

---

10 In the meantime, the author has revised his position on this matter, see Schmitz (2013, 97-108).

11 Characteristic for this arrangement is Husserl's statement: "E.g. the act corresponding the name *the knife on the table* is apparently a compound. The item of the whole act is a knife, the item of a part of the act is a table." (Husserl 1928, 5th examination, § 17). Translation by Martin Bastert.

12 Hume (1888, 253).

VII
SEVENTH HOUR
Freedom

At the end of this book, I deal with the problem of freedom. In view of this challenge, philosophical reflection is of the highest practical value and is absolutely necessary for humans as to how they live their lives, for, on the one hand, in this context, the moral responsibility of a person is implicated as such and also as a precondition for justified retribution. On the other hand, the desire to live in so far as it draws on one's own independent initiative, i.e. on the fact that the person matters for something as the author rather than everything playing out automatically. For centuries naturalists like La Mettrie and Nietzsche, jurists such as Franz v. Liszt, neuroscientists and materialist philosophers have with ideological zeal attempted to teach their audiences a "new image of man" which characterises humans as spontaneously or determinedly efficacious automata without responsibility of their own. If there were good reasons for doing so, one might consider drinking this poison, even though the consequences would be far more confusing and disabling than naïve determinists imagine. But if this "new image of man" is based on near-sighted and obscure thought, philosophy has good cause to defend against this temptation, so that people are not deceived in their self-understanding. Naturalists do, however, have an excuse for the inadequacy of their line of argument in that the philosophical tradition which since Plato has dominated the debate has encouraged such deviations from the path of thorough analysis by making the opposite mistake: by attempting to play freedom as the trump card of a self-infatuated faculty of reason and its imperiously willing stance against arbitrariness and spontaneity in human life. My examination of the problem of freedom is to correct both the mistakes of the naturalists as well as those of the idealists in equal measure. Perhaps this is the most complicated examination I have undertaken. Its results are summed up in my book *Freiheit*[1]. In the preface I ask the reader to henceforth only consider the presentation of my theory in this book as

---

1   Schmitz (2007).

the one authorised by me. I will stick to this in the sketch I present in what follows and kindly ask the reader to look up any details there.

I will not deal with the possibility of unproblematic civil, political and physical freedom which consists in the absence of coercion – a force irresistibly opposing one's own striving – and the availability of sufficient space for making decisions. I orient freedom on moral responsibility which I define as follows: a subject S is *morally responsible* for a fact F if it only depends on the relation of fact F to moral norms whether S deserves approval or disapproval for F. In that case freedom is to be understood as the existence of a non-trivial equivalent of moral responsibility, i.e. as a both necessary and sufficient condition for it which does not logically follow from the responsibility as, for instance, it itself as its both necessary and sufficient condition. Thus, the existence of freedom will have been proven if such a non-trivial equivalent – a *gestalt of freedom* – is found.

I begin by looking for a criterion of freedom, i.e. something which, independently of one's own hunches, allows for deciding whether a suggestion for a gestalt of freedom is sufficient. I find such a criterion in the common awareness of moral responsibility prevalent in contemporary ('Western') civilisation. However, I do not read this awareness off of the beliefs of people, who widely diverge from one another and can be determined by many (dogmatic) influences, but off of their typical spontaneous judgments, from which I deduce which features belong to a gestalt of freedom and which do not, even though many people are convinced of the opposite. The result of the examination is: one's own initiative, independence of this initiative and capacity for accountability are *parts of freedom*. One's own initiative consists in oneself being able to do something or not to do it, so that it does not become a fact without one doing something oneself. Independence consists in the fact that the initiative in being acted out is not directed by a power different from itself which sufficiently determines one's (not) acting. *Power* is the ability to direct something, i.e. the ability to directly set a collection of things (in the widest sense of 'something') in motion (in the widest sense, for instance, also referring to emotions), guiding and stopping this motion like the possessor of such an ability. *Capacity for accountability* is the privilege of people to accompany one's own actions with thoughts, which refer to the involved individual circumstances, norms as well as oneself. *What does not belong to freedom* is power over one's own behaviour, being able to choose and being able to act differently. *Lack of power* is seen in the following case: who has lost the ability to direct his behaviour (doing and not doing) can still resist or succumb to what is irresistible and thus be free. Cases of *not being able to choose*: *choosing* is the behaviour to knowingly restrict oneself to some (not all) possibilities despite the belief in more possibilities being available. According to the normal awareness of moral responsibility there are at least two possibilities to be free without being able to choose, i.e. morally responsible: unconscious carelessness and spontaneous actions. In the case of unconscious carelessness, there is often a lack of knowledge of the many significant behaviour options; in that case it is not a flaw of will which is morally reprehensible but a flaw of attitude, that is, the carelessness of not carefully enough having striven for knowledge of the respective possibilities. Spontaneous actions: immediate reactions, for instance bravery or cowardice in view of intimidating dangers can lead to moral approval or disapproval of who reacted, even though they reacted so fast that there was no time to take into account more than one possibility of behaving. *Not not-being able to act differently*: being able to act differently consists in being able to choose complemented by the two features of the truth of the belief and the independence of self-limiting.

At this juncture, a side glance at the debate on freedom in contemporary analytic philosophy may in one respect confirm the charge of unclear thought on the part of the naturalists. In analytic philosophy, a thorough analysis — after all, it takes its name from it – is wanting. The concept of choice is not scrutinised in the way one would expect it to be done but, as far as I know, is left undefined; a consequence of this is that not being able to act differently is equated with causal determinism and the possibility is ignored that while causal determinism is incompatible with freedom, because it cancels the independence of initiative, such an incompatibility does not apply to not-being able to, which does lack the ability to choose unnecessary for freedom, but not yet necessarily independent initiative.

By showing that independent initiative is a necessary condition of every gestalt of freedom, the relevance of the problem of freedom is expanded to include the justification of the desire to live in so far as it depends on the confidence of a human that their engagement and their independent initiative matter and that events are not impervious to what they can do or not. The resignation that one's own engagement is pointless would rob the desire to live of its energy and vitality. It is of no use to point out that it is contrary to one's own interest to just sit back: this is the objection to lazy reason already known since antiquity. In this manner, at best an impulse can be generated which is immediately inhibited by the pointlessness of engagement, and then a human makes an experience akin to what happens to a car when one, at the same time, brakes and accelerates: it starts swerving and loses track.

The naturalist denial of freedom rests on two pillars. One is the claim of causal determination of all human behaviour by means of brain processes boisterously propounded in public by materialist scientists. In dealing with it, one needs to epistemologically examine the breadth of scientific knowledge at a fundamental level; I have done so in *Freiheit*[2], but here I will leave it at pointing out that it would lie beyond the scope of the present enterprise to go into the complexities of the matter. The other pillar consists in the dilemma of a choice between determinism and indeterminism taken up again by analytic philosophy, that is, if it is conceived of as a complete disjunction, as an unavoidable dichotomy of two alternatives. For both are deadly for independent initiative. Determinism cancels independence, since external direction is taken to the point that the initiative itself, be it only submission or resistance in relation to what is unavoidable, is subject to a directedness by something alien. Indeterminism cancels initiative, since events that are directed by nothing cannot be done or not done, for then one would direct them, possibly even by doing nothing. This also holds true for an initiative of one's own not directed by anything, a person's doing it himself which in turn was not directed by his initiative, for that would be a mere insertion, such as a spontaneous verbal outburst, a not-doing-oneself and thus a foiled doing by oneself.

Analytic philosophy in its present state resigns in regard to the dilemma of the choice between determinism and indeterminism either by declaring freedom impossible or, since escaping into indeterminism appears to be fruitless, fitting it into determinism (so-called compatibilism). The compatibilist has no idea into which noose he is putting his head, because he has not conceptually analysed choice. Determinst conviction bars choice, for from this it follows that a person always only has one choice of behaving, that is, the one which he is determined to choose; but being convinced of having more than one option of how to behave is a necessary part of choosing and an honestly convinced determinist would, in view of a challenge, have to be of the conviction that he has just one, but not just one possibility of taking a stance toward it. One cannot impute such

---

2   Schmitz (2007, 94-105).

an obvious contradiction in his beliefs to the determinist. So he could not choose, not even from a menu in a restaurant. He could not behave rationally but only drift like a somnambulist. Also the counter-claim is void that he has to decide, since he cannot foresee how he will decide. For he does not have to decide but can just go with the flow and let things happen. A consistent indeterminist would have better chances than the determinist. First, nothing prevents him from believing in more than one possibility of behaving. While he cannot take the decision which he chooses into his own hands, for it would no longer be undetermined if he took the initiative in so doing, he might in a limited sense be able to restrict himself by handing the decision to a – perhaps good – inspiration which comes to him without any sense of guidance.

So if freedom is to pass between the Scylla of determinism and the Charybdis of indeterminism, in any case it will, as independent initiative, have to be a kind of causality. As such, the problem of freedom becomes entangled with that of causality. The latter concept is obscure and cannot be fully elucidated conceptually; nonetheless it is a necessary part of normal life experience. To a cause belong the two features of active causation – given as undeniable experience in suffering the causality of half-things – and the sufficiency of causation for success. Cause and success or effect have to be seen as facts and not as things or events, at least in the context of the problem of freedom. There are two reasons for this: 1. The connection of cause and effect can only be represented by a causal sentence which connects two propositions by means of conjunctions such as "because" or "since"; each of these propositions represents a fact and only in this manner is it possible to clearly demarcate what belongs to the cause and what to the effect. 2. There is moral responsibility also for things not done, so these, too, have to be independent initiatives and causes if freedom exists, but this can only be the case if they are facts; for no event, no thing can consist in something not being done, but a fact very well can. But in a figurative sense events, too, can be causes, that is, if the cause consists in the fact that the event exists. A person cannot directly be a cause but only an *agent* by means of a quality which is the cause. This quality has to be intimately connected with the person in order to be sufficient for initiative; it cannot consist in any superficial feature such as the number of hairs on a head. An initiative that took place without being caused, without a causal connection to a person, would also not be intimate enough. Thus the notion of agentive causality, which ascribes moral responsibility to such an uncaused initiative, is de-valued. Between the two features of the cause, the active causation and the sufficiency for success, there is a great difference in the necessary extent of the cause. For sufficiency, usually a great amount of further circumstances is necessary, in the case of the murder of Caesar, for instance, apart from the murderous actions of the conspirators, also the quality of the intermediate space filled by air and the vulnerability of Caesar's body. However, in the case of initiative, that somebody does something themselves, the active core is, restricted to the author and his authorship. For the sufficiency for success, in most cases this triggering cause, however, is merely a small part of the complete causal chain.

Now the examination has reached the point at which we can tackle the decisive question whether freedom can be saved, whether it is possible to bring it past the Scylla and Charybdis of determinism and indeterminism. If this fails, we will have lost moral responsibility as well as the human desire to live in so far as it is founded on the confidence that it matters whether a person does something himself and not just lets it happen to him. In case we were left only with determinism, (in the conviction that any choice and thus rational behaviour is right,) all executive self-control would have become impossible. (If so-called determinists do not let on such flaws, this only shows that their commitment to determinism has not fully sunken in.) Determinism blocks the independence of initiative in that each fact is determined by other facts; indeterminism cancels initiative itself, for if a fact is completely uncaused, then also its author cannot have caused it. But there is also a third possibility, that is, self-causation in which a fact is the cause of itself. In this case it is not uncaused as in indeterminism, but it also need not be caused by other facts. There is not the slightest indication of such self-causation in the area of objective facts. Will in particular is unsuitable to such self-causation, since will always strives beyond itself for success. So freedom as the self-causation of independent initiative cannot be free will, in any case, at least not specifically; by means of other features, not conceptually belonging to will, this, too, could possibly be free. In the area of objective facts and in view of the uniqueness of will, here, too, freedom is nowhere to be found.

Our prospects are much better if we turn to the subjective facts of affective/emotional involvement. Affective involvement has the passive side of being affected by something. But merely passive affectedness would not be affective in the sense of emotional involvement; this only happens if the person affected emotionally takes centre stage, i.e. he has to somehow participate, become involved in what affects him. In the fifth hour I have shown for the case of affective involvement in emotions, for 'being in the grip of emotions', that even an initial falling into the impulse of the emotion is a part of it before a person can, succumbing or resisting, be in its grip. In the case of embodied stirrings without being in the grip of an emotion, the leeway for initial participation is usually greater but hardly is missing, for instance, in the case of in the case of hunger, by grumpily, patiently, whiningly or aggressively suffering it. This active side of affective involvement, which is inseparably intertwined with suffering the involvement, I call the *stance* invested in affective involvement. Only by means of it is the subjectivity of affective involvement sparked or provided. Without this initially non-arbitrary entanglement of the self additionally shaped by the person's engagement, affectedness would be a neutral event which the person affected could only watch like an alien observer. This really is the case in emotional paralysis as described by Bälz and others[3]. In the case of overwhelming catastrophes, which, like earthquakes, war time events or plane crashes, emotionally demand too much of an individual, he can become paralysed; the person, compos mentis, looks down on his situation and, as though he were standing beside himself, nothing that happens moves him anymore. The affectedness is still experienced, but the person affected no longer becomes involved; his stance becomes detached. So the attitude is the active cause of the subjectivity for the person involved and thus of the subjective facts for him. He himself is one of these, understood as the fact of his existence. While someone's stance (as a fact) is not generally sufficient for the facts subjective to them, it is for itself, for every fact is sufficient for itself. So in the relation of a stance to itself both features of causation are combined, sufficiency as well as causal activity for all subjective facts of what is intended and thus for themselves. Thus the self-causation sought after has been found. As the independent initiative of someone, the stance is suitable to being self-causation in the field of subjective facts and, in case he is capable of accountability as a person, fulfils the requirements of a gestalt of freedom in such a manner that one can claim: *a personal and accountable human is morally responsible in virtue of his stance.*

This conclusion would be premature if the facts subjective for someone were not self-caused or brought about in affective involvement, but only were otherwise objective facts to which a pinch of subjectivity was added. But this is impossible, as has already been seen in (III). Facts subjective

---

3   Schmitz (2007, 66-69).

for someone are always richer than objective facts which can only be obtained by grinding down subjectivity. The former cannot be had simply by adding something. This is even true for causality. No subjective fact can have an objective cause, for then it could be characterised as an effect of the latter and the fact that this characterisation obtains would yet again be an objective fact with respect to which it would remain unclear whether one was dealing with oneself or something of one's own; for, as I have stated in the third hour, there is nothing in objective facts that indicates that we are dealing with me and not Alexander the Great. Only by finding myself in subjective facts of my affective involvement before all objective facts and by extracting objective facts from these by grinding down subjectivity is there good reason to say that I am Herrmann Schmitz and no one else. This state of affairs is suitable to rejoining to an objection one has made against me, i.e. that a stance can be just as causally determined as any other event in the world. An example that is time and again used is that of Phineas Gage through whose head a complete iron rod was driven during a rock-blasting accident, destroying much of his brain's left frontal lobe. Afterwards he changed from being a solid, reliable worker to an erratic, lying and treacherous outsider without having suffered any intellectual impairment. The objective fact is undeniable that in a complex of events and states to which one applies the name "Phineas Gage", a different stance was effected by the accident. But this is not true of the subjective fact which Gage and only Gage could have articulated thus: "I, Phineas Gage, used to be a man of reliable stance, but now this has been thoroughly shaken." This fact subjective for Phineas Gage is of a very different kind and cannot be grasped by means of the objective fact of the accident.

So human freedom is not freedom of will but freedom of stance, in which the will, in so far as it participates in affective involvement and is imbued by the attitude, can be free though, but no more than hunger or pain. One could long since have become aware of the fact that moral responsibility as deserving (dis)approval and thus freedom as its non-trivial equivalent are not merely tied to activities of willing but can also apply to stance without participation of the will. This is true of joyous Schadenfreude, envious denigration, joy about someone's suffering (also without Schadenfreude), which deserve to be morally reprimanded as stances, but it would require a stretch to re-interpret them as acts of willing (to which they can, however, be connected). In the case of unconscious carelessness, such re-interpretation is out of the question, since unconsciously doing something entails that the person doing it does not bring to awareness what he should have done and thus cannot even will doing it. Nonetheless, unconscious carelessness can amount to serious guilt, but as a flaw in attitude by being light-hearted or coarse. We are indebted to Nicolai Hartmann for having found the restriction of moral freedom to freedom of will to be too narrow and having reminded us of stance, but only to quickly pass over it and not return to it again, since the expression "Willensfreiheit" [freedom of will] has become common parlance[4].

Now that we have shown up a gestalt of freedom, we still have to examine the relation of freedom to power. Here we can no longer be dealing with the power of will but only with the power of stance. The latter depends on whether it can cause something beyond itself without which it would not have occurred. So if this is not the case, a free attitude is powerless, but still free and a source of moral responsibility; for a human capable of accountability, by means of his attitude, remains responsible for his attitude. But there would be no more encouragement with such resignation that everything happens to a person without his fresh engagement out of his own initiative. Effects of attitude and only of attitude cannot be proven, but there is also no reason not to assume that they exist. One might consider as such a reason a determinism which robbed initiative of independence and replaced it by external control. I have disproven total determinism according to which everything in the future is determined down to the last detail in *Freiheit* (pp. 88-94) by using an argument based on the proof put forward in the fourth hour that not everything is singular[5]. A remaining option is a form of partial determinism, for instance, with respect to scientifically measurable properties. However, the claim of science to provide causal explanation (rather than prognosis) of the processes in the life world of our spontaneous life experience is questionable. One has (and still is) conducting experiments that are intended to prove that acts of willing are determined by foregoing brain processes, but what an experiment would look like with which one could show that all possible consequences of the facts of attitude subjective for someone (if only in the field of objective facts) by means of scientific measurement of the brain or other sources is utterly inconceivable. For this reason there is no good reason to dislodge the belief that humans can change the world by acting freely, which is a precondition for the desire to live. But one cannot do

---

4   Hartmann (1949, 622 f.).
5   See Schmitz (2013, 69-76).

so with the power of a will free to decide. This option is concealed by the dilemma of will as locked between determinism and indeterminism. If freedom has any power at all, then in this manner: *not what humans deliberate to do but what they freshly insert as stance into their affective involvement in the moment, and thus the way in which they, as affectively involved persons, are engaged in the matter, gives them causal power out of independent initiative.*

In this sentence our brief presentation of the basic ideas of New Phenomenology has reached its goal. If I take a look at the gains of New Phenomenology, I see it spread out in two separate directions: one releases vast amounts of life experience from the prison house (box) of the psychologistic-reductionist-introjectionist objectification of the felt body, of embodied communication, of emotions as atmospheres, of significant situations and meaningful impressions, of half-things/entities. The other direction aims to firmly root subjectivity in subjective facts and other subjective meanings (non-actual states of affairs, programmes, problems). In this manner the threateningly expanding ironist age is not robbed of its habitat but at least of its theoretic foundation. This age dawned when humans had, by means of scientific singularism, so thoroughly atomised and neutralised their experience and themselves as conscious subjects (in Hume's view becoming mere bundles of perception) that they could no longer recognise themselves. Then the question arose: "Where am I?" In philosophy this question was first posed by Johann Gottlieb Fichte. But since he and his contemporaries believed all facts to be neutral or objective ones in which they could not recognise themselves, they themselves were locked in a floating state (the floating of imagination according to Fichte) above or between all facts. Of this Friedrich Schlegel made romantic irony as the versatility of being able to turn away from everything and thus also to everything, of being able to choose any position/point of view. Thus he heralded the new ironist era, which in the 19th century was enacted by the dandy in aristocratic understatement but has now become vulgarised as coolness in front of TV or the computer. The discovery of subjective facts of affective involvement corrects the error at the source of this development and thus opens our eyes for a possible end of the ironist age, not, of course, for a prepared path to stooping the tide of an ascent to perfected frivolity in the tracks of Max Stirner. Furthermore, the discovery of subjective facts offers an opportunity to resolve the age-old problem of freedom which has been so twisted by intellectually arrogant idealists that naturalists adopted the opposite extreme of denying freedom altogether or compatibilistically throwing it to the determinist dogs. Since a justified education of humans about their freedom is of the utmost importance for their ability to live, both for their desire to do so as well as for their belief in moral responsibility (including the preparedness for retribution), it is justified to close this book with an hour dedicated to freedom.

BIBLIOGRAPHY

Aeschylus
1900 *Choephoroe*, in: *The Oresteia of Aschylus*, tr. and ed. by George C. W. Warr, George Allen, London.

Diogenes Laertius
1925 *Lives of Eminent Philosophers*, vol. 2, tr. by Robert Drew Hicks, William Heinemann/G. P. Putnam's Sons, London/New York.

Freeman, K.
1948 *Ancilla to the Pre-Socratic Philosophers: a Complete Translation of the Fragments in Diels, Fragmente der Vorsokratiker*, Blackwell, Oxford.

Gabriel, G. et al.
1976 *Gottlob Freges wissenschaftlicher Briefwechsel*, Felix Meiner, Hamburg.

Goethe, J. W.
1908 *Faust*, tr. by Abraham Hayward, Hutchinson, London.

Hartmann, N.
1949 *Ethik*, 3rd ed., Walter de Gruyter, Berlin.

Hegel, G. W. F.
1952 *Briefe von und an Hegel*, vol. 1, Felix Meiner, Hamburg.

Hume, D.
1888 *A Treatise of Human Nature*, ed. by Lewis Amherst Selby-Bigge, Clarendon Press, Oxford (reprint 1951).

Husserl, E.
1928 *Logische Untersuchungen*, vol. 2, part 1, 4th edition, Niemeyer, Halle an der Saale.
1983 *Ideas Pertaining to a Pure Phenomenology and to a Phenomenological Philosophy*, first book, tr. by F. Kersten, Martinus Nijhoff, The Hague.

Kant, I.
1942 *Preisschrift über die Fortschritte der Metaphysik*, in: *Kant's gesammelte Schriften*, vol. 20, ed. by Preußische Akademie der Wissenschaften, Walter de Gruyter, Berlin.
1998 *Critique of Pure Reason*, tr. and ed. by Paul Guyer and Allen W. Wood, Cambridge University Press, Cambridge.

Luther, M.
1908 *Large Catechism*, tr. by John Nicholas Lenker, The Luther Press, Minneapolis.

Metzger, W.
1975 *Psychologie*, 5th ed., Steinkopff, Darmstadt.

Nietzsche, F.
1950 *Thus Spake Zarathustra*, tr. by Thomas Common, The Modern Library, New York.

Pfister-Ammende, M.
1949 *Psychologische Erfahrungen mit sowjetrussischen Flüchtlingen in der Schweiz*, in: *Die Psychohygiene*. Grundlagen und Ziele, ed. by Maria Pfister-Ammende, Hans Huber, Bern.

Sartre, J.-P.
1943 *L'être et le néant*, Gallimard, Bibliothèque des idées, Paris.

Schmitz, H.
1959 *Goethes Altersdenken im problemgeschichtlichen Zusammenhang*, Bouvier, Bonn (reprint 2008).
1966 *System der Philosophie*, vol. II, part 2: Der Leib im Spiegel der Kunst, Bouvier, Bonn (reprint 2005).
1967 *System der Philosophie*, vol. III: Der Raum, part 1: Der leibliche Raum, Bouvier, Bonn (reprint 2005).
1969 *System der Philosophie*, vol. III: Der Raum, part 2: Der Gefühlsraum, Bouvier, Bonn (reprint 2005).
1973, *System der Philosophie*, vol. III: Der Raum, part 3: Der Rechtsraum, Bouvier, Bonn (reprint 2005).
1977 *System der Philosophie*, vol. III: Der Raum, part 4: Das Göttliche und der Raum, Bouvier, Bonn (reprint 2005).
1980 System der Philosophie, vol. IV: Die Person, Bouvier, Bonn [reprint 2005].
1993 *Die Liebe*, Bouvier, Bonn.
1994 *Neue Grundlagen der Erkenntnistheorie*, Bouvier, Bonn.
1997 *Höhlengänge*, de Gruyter, Berlin (reprint 2015).
2007 *Freiheit*, Karl Alber, Freiburg/München.
2008a *Logische Untersuchungen*, Karl Alber, Freiburg/München.
2008b Hermann Schmitz, *Leib und Gefühl*, 3rd ed., Aisthesis, Bielefeld/Locarno.

2011 *Der Leib*, Walter de Gruyter, Berlin/Boston.
2012 *Das Reich der Normen*, Karl Alber, Freiburg/München.
2013 *Kritische Grundlegung der Mathematik*, Karl Alber, Freiburg/München.
2014 *Phänomenologie der Zeit*, Karl Alber, Freiburg/München.
Schneider, K.
1950 *Klinische Psychopathologie*, 3rd ed., Thieme, Stuttgart.

Schopenhauer, A.
1863 *Von ihm. Über ihn. Briefe und Nachlasstücke*, ed. by Julius Frauenstädt, A. W. Hayn, Berlin.

Thomae, H.
1960 *Der Mensch in der Entscheidung*, J. A. Barth, München.

Weyl, H.
1968, *Gesammelte Abhandlungen*, vol. 4, Springer, Berlin/Heidelberg/New York (first published in 1955).

Wlosok, A.
1980 *Über die Rolle der Scham in der römischen Rechtskultur*, in: Grazer Beiträge 9 (1980), pp. 155-72, reprinted in: Antonie Wlosok, *Res humanae – res divinae. Kleine Schriften*, ed. by Eberhard Heck and Ernst A. Schmidt, Heidelberg 1990.

GLOSSARY

A short overview over some German terms introduced by Hermann Schmitz or used by him in a specific manner

GERMAN	TRANSLATION BY R. O. MÜLLAN/M. BASTERT	EXPLANATION / ALTERNATIVE TRANSLATION / EXAMPLE[1]
Atmosphäre	atmosphere	Unbound occupation of a surfaceless space in the region of what is experienced as present.
Antrieb, vitaler	vital drive	The axis of bodily dynamism.
Augenblick, absoluter	absolute moment	absolute now of sth.
Ausleibung	excorporation	Trance-like states in which the contraction of the felt body sustained by the contracting tendency phases over into expansion.
Bedeutsamkeit, binnendiffuse	internally diffuse meaningfulness	A meaningfulness which is diffuse, because within it not everything (or possibly even nothing) is singular.
Bedeutung, subjektive	subjective meaning	A meaning that can be said by one person at the most.
Bedeutung, objektive	objective meaning	A meaning that can be said by anyone as long as he knows enough about it and can speak well enough.
Betroffensein, affektives	affective involvement	being deeply affected by sth.
Bewegungssuggestion	suggestion of motion	embodied bridging quality, e.g. rhythm
Bewussthaber	conscious subject	Sb. or sth that has the ability of self-ascription (conscious life).

---

1   In case that no additional explanation, translation or example is provided, the English term is believed to be sufficiently self-explanatory and thus only included in this list for the sake of completeness.

Bewussthaben	having-in-consciousness	relational consciousness
Bewusstsein	consciousness	The having-in-consciousness of the conscious subject who is conscious of something.
Brückenqualitäten	bridging qualities	Qualities that can be noticed in one's own felt body as well as they can be perceived in encounters with others (whether at rest or in motion).
Dauer, intensive	duration	
Dynamik, leibliche	embodied dynamism	One of the two most important sources of situations, the other one being embodied communication. Its axis is the vital drive with its extensions by means of privative expansion and privative contraction towards expandedness or contactedness.
Einleibung, antagonistische	antagonistic encorporation	Embodied communication in which a shared vital drive arises as a result of attending to a partner in communication.
Einleibung, einseitige antagonistische	one-sided antagonistic encorporation	An encorporation in which the dominant and binding contracting pole of the shared vital drive remains on one side.
Einleibung, solidarische	solidary encorporation	A shared vital drive connects many individuals without anyone turning to any other.
Einleibung, wechselseitige antagonistische	mutual antagonistic encorporation	The source of spontaneous certainty to be dealing with another conscious subject (which can occasionally also be misleading).

einzeln	singular	Sth. that increases a number by 1.
Eigensphäre	private inner sphere	Similar to the term "soul", this term refers to a locked-off sphere containing the entirety of personal experience.
Eigenwelt, persönliche	personal idiosyncratic world	The personal idiosyncratic world of a person contains all meanings which are subjective for him and everything for which the (factual or non-factual) state of affairs that they exist is of this kind.
Emanzipation, personale	personal emancipation	The singularisation and neutralisation of meanings with the consequence that what is idiosyncratic can set itself off from what is neutral and alien and thus personality solidifies and develops.
Engung und Weitung	contraction and expansion	The two intertwined tendencies that constitute the vital drive, which is the axis of the idiosyncratic dynamic of the felt body.
fremd	alien	
Fremdwelt, persönliche	personal alien world	The personal alien world contains all meanings which have lost subjectivity for a person by means of neutralisation (i.e. objectivisation) and everything for which the (factual or non-factual) state of affairs that they exist is of this kind.
Gattung	type	In this juncture, "type" refers to everything, of which sth. can be the case.
Gefühle	emotions	

Gegenwart, primitive	primitive present	Primitive present is a rare exceptional state that possibly is never reached in its purest form with full consciousness, but that, within contraction, is latently sketched out as a component of the vital drive.
Halbding	half-thing	Half-things differ from full-things in two ways: 1. Their duration can be interrupted without there being any point in asking what they did in the meantime. 2. Whereas causality generally is tripartite, subdivided into cause (e.g. a falling stone), influence (e.g. impact) and effect (e.g. the destruction or dislodgement of the object hit), the causality of half-things is bipartite and immediate in that cause and influence overlap.
Individuum	individual	An individual is a singular case which is not subdivided into subordinate cases.
Leib	felt body	"The felt body is a feeling body – its mode of existence cannot be separated from its becoming manifest to the conscious subject in specific kinds of corporeal feeling." (Jan Slaby)

| leiblich | bodily/embodied | Bodily/embodied is whatever someone feels in the vicinity (not always within the boundaries) of their body as belonging to themselves and without drawing on the senses, in particular, seeing and touching as well as the perceptual body schema (the habitual conception of one's own body) derived from the experiences made by means of the senses. |

MIMESIS GROUP
www.mimesis-group.com

MIMESIS INTERNATIONAL
www.mimesisinternational.com
info@mimesisinternational.com

MIMESIS EDIZIONI
www.mimesisedizioni.it
mimesis@mimesisedizioni.it

ÉDITIONS MIMÉSIS
www.editionsmimesis.fr
info@editionsmimesis.fr

MIMESIS COMMUNICATION
www.mim-c.net

MIMESIS EU
www.mim-eu.com

Printed by
Digital-Team – Fano (PU)
September 2019